"*The Lord Bless You* brought me great joy. It is written in a beautiful, flowing and accessible manner that immediately put me at ease. Hallelujah! It isn't religious! It's revelatory and it will also give you joy and purpose when you discover that our God is loving and kind and generous and longs to completely bless His people—YOU!"

Kathie Lee Gifford, entertainer, author
and imperfect follower of Jesus

"A fun read. Terry Smith unpacks the meaning of three powerful words that launch God's purpose of human flourishing. *The Lord Bless You* takes us on a devotional journey into God's attitude toward our world and the people who live in it, and how we can partner with God to experience that purpose—a life of blessing!"

A. R. Bernard, pastor, Christian
Cultural Center, New York

"*The Lord Bless You* is like a notification that unexpectedly appears on the home screen of your phone reminding you of something you would have easily overlooked. Of all the intentions that God has for those made in His image, it's as if we get amnesia when it comes to His great desire to bless us. This is a deeply meaningful book everyone should read—it is biblically saturated with evidence that will make us hear what the Lord wants to do even when we haven't sneezed."

Wayne Francis, pastor, Life Church New York;
co-author, *God and Race: A Guide for Moving
Beyond Black Fists and White Knuckles*

"At a time when we desperately need it, Terry Smith has unwrapped and put the spotlight on the life-changing, eternal power of blessing. This fresh, inspiring 28-day journey teaches us how to receive blessing, give blessing, create an environment of blessing and leave a legacy of blessing!"

Kevin Gerald, pastor, Champions Centre; author, *Naked and Unafraid: 5 Keys to Abandon Smallness, Overcome Criticism, and Be All You Are Meant to Be*

"Pastor Terry does it again! This book is inspirational and aspirational as it takes you through a 28-day journey of what it really means to be blessed by God as well as what it means to be a true blessing to others. Thank you, Terry, for being a blessing to our members at TLCC."

Roman Oben, twelve-year NFL player; Super Bowl XXXVII champion; vice president of football operations, National Football League

THE
LORD

Bless
You

THE LORD

Bless You

A 28-DAY JOURNEY TO EXPERIENCE
GOD'S EXTRAVAGANT BLESSINGS

TERRY A. SMITH

Chosen

a division of Baker Publishing Group
Minneapolis, Minnesota

© 2023 by Terry A. Smith

Published by Chosen Books
Minneapolis, Minnesota
www.chosenbooks.com

Chosen Books is a division of
Baker Publishing Group, Grand Rapids, Michigan

Printed in the United States of America

Library of Congress Cataloging-in-Publication Data
Names: Smith, Terry A., 1962– author.
Title: The Lord bless you : a 28-day journey to experience God's extravagant blessings / Terry A. Smith.
Description: Minneapolis, Minnesota : Chosen Books, a division of Baker Publishing Group, [2023] | Includes bibliographical references.
Identifiers: LCCN 2022025828 | ISBN 9780800762827 (hardcover) | ISBN 9781493439317 (ebook)
Subjects: LCSH: Spirituality—Christianity—Miscellanea.
Classification: LCC BV4501.3 .S65674 2023 | DDC 269/.6—dc23/eng/20220708
LC record available at https://lccn.loc.gov/2022025828

Cover design by Studio Gearbox

Author represented by The Fedd Agency, Inc.

Baker Publishing Group publications use paper produced from sustainable forestry practices and post-consumer waste whenever possible.

23 24 25 26 27 28 29   7 6 5 4 3 2 1

To Two Great Men

My dad, Delton G. Smith
You showed me how to go on a faith adventure.
Your memory may now be gone,
but I remember it well.

My father-in-law, Donald "Poppy" Deck
You inspired me to dream of Eden.
We will meet you there.

CONTENTS

Bless You

AN INTRODUCTION

Have you ever wondered why people say the words *bless you* when someone near them sneezes? In my part of the world, you could be walking by a stranger in Central Park in New York City, be surrounded by rabid fans watching a baseball game at Yankee Stadium or be jammed in a subway car full of harried commuters, but if you sneeze, strangers, fans or commuters will all respond immediately with a loud, "Bless you!" It is a nice gesture, but where did this *bless-you* thing come from?

Nearly every culture in the world has some way of wishing sneezers well. The phrase *God bless you* was enshrined by an edict of Pope Gregory the Great all the way back in AD 600. An epidemic of the Bubonic Plague was spreading rampantly, and sneezing was an obvious symptom of this dreaded, often fatal, sickness. So Gregory ordered everyone within earshot of a sneeze to immediately utter a prayer asking God to save the person from the plague: God bless you.

I like the idea that when a person manifests a symptom of illness, those around them offer a prayer: "The Lord bless you. May He deliver you from sickness and bring you health."

Odd as it may seem, the phrase *bless you* captures the heart of God for people in ways both cosmically large and day-to-day-detail small. The very first description in Scripture of God's relationship with the people He made is, "God blessed them." I imagine God standing in the Garden passionately declaring His unconditional love to them, telling them how much He valued them and swearing to do good to them and to help them do good in this world.

It strikes me that God blessed them knowing full well they were going to sneeze, they were going to fall sick and they were going to be plagued by sin. His clear desire, though, was to bless them in their innocent beginning, to bless them as much as possible after they fell sick and then to bless them completely back into the healthy and flourishing life He planned when He created them.

The Lord Bless You is a book about how much God wants to bless the people He has made. It is about how much He wants to bless you in particular, how you can embrace His blessings in your life and how you can bless the world around you. I hope to reframe the way you see everything by helping you view the world through the lens of God's zealous intention to bless you.

Regardless of your present circumstance, God wants to bless you. Whether you are spiritually healthy or spiritually sick, God wants to bless you. Whether you are overwhelmed with abundance or struggling in scarcity, God wants to bless you. Whether your relationships are whole or less than what they should be, God wants to bless you. Whether you are vocationally satisfied or are still trying to figure out what you really want to do, God wants to bless you. Wherever you are in your life, you need only believe in Him, trust His good intentions toward you, accept what He has done through Jesus to bring you back into His full blessing and by His grace align your life with the way He designed life to be lived. You can absolutely experience God's blessing in every area of your life!

Words related to blessing are used more than five hundred times in the Bible. Various scholars define the word *blessing* in Scripture in similar ways. They say things such as "God's blessing on people involves His positive regard for them, the desire to see that they enjoy the truly good things in life." Or "Blessing has to do with being in favor with God and under his protection and care." It also has been defined as "multidimensional flourishing . . . physically, psychologically, socially, spiritually." These descriptions of blessing are beautiful and true.

For this book, however, I will define *blessing* as this: To be blessed is to be in harmonious relationship with God who wants to do good in us, to us and through us.

We might say the whole story of Scripture is about God's plan to redeem us from the curse and restore us to the blessing He planned in the beginning. Yes, humanity did fall ill. Yes, the world, though beautiful, is still plagued. And yes, this has an impact on our lives in ways large and small every day. God, however, has not changed His mind about what He wants for you. God wants to bless you.

The Lord Bless You is organized into four parts with seven short, inspirational chapters in each part. Part 1, Blessing, will help you better understand and experience blessing. Part 2, Purpose, will help you better understand and live your purpose, knowing that blessing is inextricably connected to destiny fulfillment. Part 3, People, will help you better understand and practice God's plan for you to powerfully bless others. Part 4, Gratitude, will help you better understand how intentional gratitude enhances the probability of more blessing in and through your life.

I encourage you to engage and enjoy *The Lord Bless You* in whatever way works best for you. I do invite you to consider reading and reflecting on one chapter a day for 28 days. As you may have heard, 28 days is an optimal period in which to establish a new habit. I pray you will create a habit of blessing in your life. The Lord bless you!

BLESSING

one

Adam Sneezed

was mesmerized as I stood staring at Michelangelo's AD 1512 masterpiece, *The Creation of Adam* that was on the ceiling of the Sistine Chapel in Rome. The artist depicts God reaching out of heaven and touching the outstretched hand of a perfect man who was made in God's image. This painting is so famous you can probably picture it in your mind. I can easily imagine the Lord saying "I bless you" to this flawless specimen of a human being.

Several years after I saw *The Creation of Adam*, I visited the J. Paul Getty Museum in Los Angeles, and I saw John-François Millet's painting *Man with a Hoe*. This painting, first displayed in Paris in 1863, depicts a large, dirty, brutish man bent over a hoe attempting to turn rocky, thistle-ridden soil into a productive field. He is clearly exhausted by his backbreaking labor. Millet was a religious fatalist who believed that people were tragically condemned to bear a heavy burden. As I looked at Millet's weary man, my mind flashed back to Michelangelo's Adam. I thought, *Is this what Adam looked like after the Fall?* And my heart broke. I believed that God could bless the Adam of Eden, but could He bless the Adam in the wilderness who was broken by the Fall?

The first thing God said to the first human beings was, "Bless you." But then they sneezed. God gave Adam and Eve free will. They were given a choice as to whether they would live in God's full blessing or go their own way. They chose their own way, and therefore chose a curse rather than a blessing. The plague of sin was introduced to the human race, and the whole world fell sick. Adam went from the wonder of meeting God every day and working and caring for the Garden of Eden and its limitless bounty to being a profusely sweating, exhausted man who was trying to break up rocky soil in a barren wilderness. Michelangelo's glorious Adam became Millet's *Man with a Hoe*. Can God bless this guy?

That burdened guy is us. Making mistakes. Suffering pain. Torn by broken relationships. Fighting burnout. Slammed by world events. Far too often lonely, anxious or sad. Can God bless troubled us as we attempt to navigate the terrain of a damaged world? The answer quite simply is yes. He wants to. He can. And if we let Him, He will.

Before humanity fell sick, God had prepared the cure. He stood in the Garden and looked at the man and woman, newly cursed with an awareness of evil, and said, "I'll be back." He told them that a man would come from the woman who would reverse the curse and restore the blessing. And history began moving forward, eagerly waiting for that man to appear.

And at the perfect moment in the fullness of time, Jesus came and did what needed to be done to redeem humanity—to win back what had been lost—and to reconcile us to God and His blessing. If we believe in Jesus and are in relationship with Him, we can live and grow in that blessing despite the brokenness in us and around us. In the letter to the Romans in the New Testament, Paul said:

> For if, by the trespass of the one man [Adam], death reigned through that one man, how much more will those who receive God's abundant provision of grace and of the gift of righteousness reign in life through the one man, Jesus Christ!

To live in the blessing God wanted for us in the beginning does not mean that life is perfect. We are still broken people in a broken world. The more we know Jesus and grow to be like Him, however, the more we live like the Adam who was blessed, and the less we live like the Adam who was cursed. The more we submit to God's rule in our lives, the more we reign in life through Jesus Christ. We will not experience the totality of this reality until the age to come, but we can taste it now.

Because of Jesus, the wounded God-image in us is being healed. Because of Jesus, the world around us—the world we influence—looks more like Eden and less like wilderness. We should live with an expectation that everything in our life is becoming more and more the way God wanted it to be in the beginning and wants it to be now.

Check this out: God blessed Adam and Eve, and then they got sick. Did God change His mind about what He wanted? Of course not. Move forward. God started over with Noah and his family. Guess what God does? "Then God blessed Noah and his sons." Move forward. God makes a covenant with Abraham through whom Jesus would come to redeem the world. Guess what He says to Abraham?

> "I will make you into a great nation, and I will bless you; I will make your name great, and you will be a blessing. I will bless those who bless you, and whoever curses you I will curse; and all peoples on earth will be blessed through you."

Then we are told that at the end of his life, "Abraham was now very old, and the Lord had blessed him in every way." Move forward. Abraham had a son named Isaac. Guess what happened? "The Lord blessed him." Move forward. Isaac had a son named Jacob who was so insistent to continue the line of blessing that he had an encounter with God and prayed for God's blessing. And guess what happened next? The Lord "blessed him there."

Move forward thousands of years. Move forward to now. Move forward to you. What do you think God wants to do to you? You may feel broken, burdened and perhaps even exhausted as you live in a world that far too often seems to be plagued. But God wants to bless you. And He wants you to become more like that first man or woman in the place of paradise in the beginning before the world fell sick. And because of Jesus you can.

Scripture tells us that faith in Jesus and living with an expectation of God's blessing is essential to being blessed in every way. Do you really believe God wants to bless you?

---

two

Good God

The most important theme of all of Scripture may very well be how much God wants to bless you— and all of humanity. God's desire to bless us is most certainly the central theme of Genesis, and this is no small thing. Genesis is the book of beginnings. It tells us what God wanted us to know about His intentions for the world and the people He created.

Genesis was not written in a vacuum. It is the oldest part of our Bible, but it was not the oldest literature in the ancient Near East. There is a body of mythological writings from Mesopotamia, Egypt and other ancient Near-Eastern cultures that predate Moses and his inspired Genesis account. These mythologies tell stories of how gods and goddesses created the world and humanity.

These gods and goddesses were totally unlike the one true God, who reveals Himself in Genesis. They warred against one another, were not constrained by a moral code, had relations with one another, procreated and brought into being men and women who became slaves tasked with the menial and unfulfilling work that the gods and goddesses wanted them to do. Moses wrote Genesis to tell a better story about a better God and His better plan for humanity.

Genesis was not written to be a science manual. Its intention is not to tell us the detailed how, where and when of Creation. Its intention is to tell us the who and why. God is the who, and the why is that He wanted to create a community of people He could be in relationship with and bless, and with whom He could partner to spread His glory throughout the earth.

So the literature that existed before Genesis told a bad story of a pantheon of gods and goddesses and their purposes for human beings. The best scholarship indicates that Moses began writing Genesis in the fifteenth century BC during the exodus of the Jews from their four-hundred-year sojourn in Egypt. It is well within the realm of probability that God's chosen people had heard these "bad" stories while in Egypt.

But God used Moses to set the record straight. He had a good story to tell. Through him, God said, *Those stories you heard in Egypt are not true. Here is who I am. Here is why I made you.* His story is about one God in three persons living in perfect unity. His story is about a good God who created human beings in His own image. His story is a story of love and purpose and meaning. And again, the very first thing said about God's interaction with human beings all the way back at the very beginning is that "God blessed them."

Imagine the first people who heard this better story all those millennia ago. I can almost hear a cosmic sigh of relief. "Wait. God is good? God wants to be in relationship with us? He wants to do good in us and to us and through us? God wants to bless us?"

Imagine God standing in the Garden with the first man and woman who were both created in His image, His heart overwhelmed with godly pride. His very first act was to bless them, to convey His unconditional love for them and how much He valued them and to tell them how many good things He had planned for their future. I do not know exactly how all of this happened, but I do know that this is the story God wanted to tell His people during the exodus about His relationship with the first people He created. This is the story He wants to tell us. This better story about a better God—a God who wants to bless the people He made—changed everything for them, and it changes everything for us.

We live our lives out of the stories we know, the stories we believe and the stories we tell ourselves and others.

As James Bryan Smith wrote, "All behavior is based on a narrative." If you believe in a good God who wants to do good and only good to you, it will change the way you think and live.

Just as there were other existing origin and purpose narratives that Moses needed to correct, so there are a variety of narratives that inform the way people think and live in our world today. Some stories do not include God at all, and others fail to accurately describe God the way He reveals Himself in Scripture. A God who is infinite and personal (He is an unknowable mystery who nevertheless chooses to make Himself known), transcendent and immanent (He is beyond and outside our world yet loves us enough to show up in our world), omniscient (all-knowing), sovereign (all-powerful and ultimately in control of everything) and good (the prime reality of God's character from which all other aspects of His character flow). That is the God described to us in Scripture and made known to us through Jesus Christ.

For us to live a better story with our lives, it is essential that we infuse our thoughts with God's better story and believe and act accordingly. The narrative in Scripture tells us the story of a good God who created the universe and people out of His love. It tells of a God who gave people dignity, purpose and free will. And when people decided to reject His good plan for them, He enacted a self-sacrificial plan to show up on this planet to bring people back to Him and His original good intentions. The Christian story, then, centers on God who came to earth in a person named Jesus, whose life, death, resurrection and exaltation offers us the possibility to be restored to what God wanted in the beginning. And what did God want for us in the beginning? He wanted to bless us.

I challenge you today to think about God as He is described and as He describes Himself in Scripture. Ignore the other stories you have been told. Ignore the stories you tell yourself, such as narratives that claim this universe is a cosmic accident and that life has no meaning, or that if there is a God, He does not care about someone like you. Consider the possibility that more than anything else what the infinite, personal, transcendent, immanent, omniscient, sovereign and good God most wants to do is bless you.

Do you have stories in your mind that oppose the biblical story of a good God who wants to bless you? What do you need to do to challenge those false narratives and to fill your mind with truth that leads to faith and living your best story?

three

Align Yourself

For Christmas of 2019, two of our adult children—Sumerr and Caleb—surprised my wife, Sharon, and me with the gift of a puppy we did not know we wanted. At first, we tried to politely regift him; however, we grew to hopelessly love our beautiful miniature schnauzer. A schnauzer is a German breed, so we named him Dietrich in honor of the great German pastor-theologian Dietrich Bonhoeffer. An unintended consequence of the Covid quarantine of early 2020 was that we were not able to send him to a professional trainer as we had planned. Dietrich, although well-bred and otherwise uber intelligent, missed a couple of steps in his development.

One of those steps is an understanding of the word *come*. His two favorite things in the world are to play

Frisbee and go on walks, but he will not bring me the Frisbee so I can throw it to him, and he will not come so that I can put him in a harness to leash and walk him. I like to throw him the Frisbee and take him for walks, but I spend an inordinate amount of time chasing him, which he also enjoys. I chase him so that I can do for him what he desperately wants to do and what I enjoy doing with him. If he would just respond to my call for him to come, he would align himself with my good intentions, and I would find great pleasure in giving him what he fervently desires.

This may sound a little silly, but one day, while more than a little frustrated from trying to catch Dietrich so that I could bless him, it occurred to me that this might be how God often feels about me. He passionately wants to do good to me and in me and through me, but sometimes I make it terribly difficult for Him to do what He wants to do. We must cooperate with God in order for Him to be able to bless us. We must align ourselves with His good intentions. Yes, He desires to bless us, but we must get ourselves in a position where we can be blessed.

I love the passage in Ephesians where we are told that God "has blessed us in the heavenly realms with every spiritual blessing in Christ." In the reality of the spiritual world, there already exists every spiritual blessing for those who are in relationship with Jesus. These spiritual blessings are apparently limitless, and they most certainly include things such as peace with God with the deep inner peace that follows as well as freedom from worry, fear, depression or any other negative emotion that we might feel.

And when we have spiritual blessings, such as peace with God, they leak-flow-flood into every area of our lives and significantly influence the material world around us. Jesus taught us that when things are in proper order in the depths of our soul, then everything else concerning us will be right as well. The question is, how do we appropriate these blessings that God has for us? How do we bring them from the heavenly realm into the realm of our own experience and the practicalities of the life we live now?

Several years ago, I engaged in a three-month P90X fitness challenge. There is a lot about that ninety days of extreme fitness sessions that I would prefer to forget, but the instructions for a particular drill still ring in my head. The idea of this specific exercise is to reach down to the floor on one side of your body and imagine picking something up with both hands. You are then to reach as far and as high as possible on the other side of your body to place that thing on an imaginary shelf. You are to do this over and over, even though you are already exhausted from a series of far more grueling exercises. The instructor repeatedly shouts, "Pick it up off the floor and place it on the shelf!"

When it comes to spiritual blessings that exist for us in the heavenly realm, I propose the reverse of that movement, a spiritual exercise of sorts. Name the blessing that you need or want—that God already has for you—and imagine reaching up into the heavenly realm, the world of spiritual reality that surrounds you, and bring it down into your soul. Then pause to "see" that blessing have an impact on you in some area of need and desire in your life. Reach up—grab it—bring it down. God wants you to have it. It already exists for you in the heavenly realm. You just have to appropriate it into your life. It is not that you earn it, of course, but that you align yourself with His desire and act to receive something that He has already willed.

There are three fundamentally important things we must do to take hold of the blessings God has for us and bring them into our lives.

First: We must believe. It is impossible to convey how impossible it is for God to truly bless someone who does not believe in Him and His good intentions for them. A pivot point in human history is when God chose Abraham out of everyone in the world and promised repeatedly to bless him and the world through him. Abraham connected to that promise because he "believed the LORD." And now God has chosen you, and He has promised to bless you in the way He blessed Abraham. We receive this promise, which comes by God's Spirit, through faith. Put simply, we must believe that just as God blessed Abraham in every way, He wants to bless us in every way. As Paul wrote, "So those who rely on faith are blessed along with Abraham." We bring—or more accurately perhaps, receive—this promise into our lives when we say, "I believe," and when our faith is manifested in trust and faithfulness over the long haul of our lives.

Second: We must pray according to what we believe. Prayer takes the blessings that are ours in the unseen realm of spiritual reality and makes them ours in reality in the here and now. When we pray, we are able to see things on earth align with the way things are in heaven. Part of prayer is asking God for things we want that are in agreement with what He wants. This includes His desire to bless us in every way. James taught us, "The reason you don't have what you want is that you do not ask God for it." John reminded us that our asking must be in alignment with His will. "We can be confident that he will listen to us whenever we ask him for anything in line with his will. . . . We can be sure that he will give us what we ask for."

Third: We must act in ways that convey an expectation that good things will happen in our lives. I love how Paul prayed constantly for some of his friends that God would "fulfill every good purpose of yours and every act prompted by your faith." We must act in ways that line up with what we believe and have asked for. Expect to be blessed, and act like it! What do you need today? Inner peace? Expect it. Relief from some point of pain? Expect it. A breakthrough with one of your children? Expect it. A success in your business? Expect it.

So God wants to bless you, but you must cooperate with Him to actualize His good intentions. Come to Him in faith. Ask Him for what you want and need. Act as if you expect to receive it. When you do these things, you align yourself with what God wants to do, and you move spiritual possibility into the realm of lived reality.

What is something good you need to believe for, pray for and act for today?

four

Live a Masterpiece

I n order to fully actualize a life of blessing, we must live our lives as God designed our lives to be lived.

The most famous painting in the sensational collection of works by the Dutch Masters in the Rijksmuseum in Amsterdam is Rembrandt's AD 1642 masterpiece *The Night Watch*. Rembrandt designed this painting to be nearly fourteen-and-a-half feet wide by twelve feet high. It is huge and magnificent. Yet it is not everything that it was meant to be. It was damaged when it was moved from one location to another in AD 1715.

It was deemed by its owners to be too large for the wall they wanted to place it on. So these geniuses cut off part of three sides to make *The Night Watch* fit where they wanted to display it. Imagine the thought process of these guys. "We'll just cut off a little here and a little there. That's good enough. Just hang it there." As of this writing, *The Night Watch* is valued at more than five hundred million dollars. It would have made more sense to rebuild the wall, or maybe even rebuild the entire building, rather than damage the masterpiece.

I was able to view this painting in all its glory during a three-month period in 2021 when scientists and artists collaborated to add their version of the missing pieces to the original work according to what they believed Rembrandt intended. The damaged work is fabulous, but the re-creation was abundantly more satisfying. It demonstrated what Rembrandt had actually created.

This makes me think about how God designed the world and placed people in it for purposes only known to Him, and how this perfect world was damaged by actors who did not fully appreciate the genius of the Creator's design. This world is still a beautiful place, but it is not all it was meant to be. Human beings are still glorious, but God intended so much more. It seems we might all learn a simple lesson: When it comes to God's design, do not mess with His masterpiece.

This is part of the message of Lady Wisdom—the personification of wisdom in Proverbs—when she links wisdom to a fundamental understanding of how the world was designed. She tells us that wisdom was formed before God created anything else, and that wisdom was the artist at God's side when He created His masterpiece. "I was the architect at his side. I was his constant delight, rejoicing always in his presence. And how happy I was with the world he created; how I rejoiced with the human family!"

Wisdom is saying that she can tell us how God engineered the world, what He intended for people and how, if we understand this, we can live life the way it was meant to be lived. Ultimately, wisdom is understanding how God designed the world to work and then designing our lives accordingly.

Do you ever attempt to force God's masterpiece into your reality? Do you cut a little off here and there from God's design and still expect to live your best possible life? If we want to live in the blessing God wanted for us in the beginning, then we must live life the way He designed life to be lived.

There is another passage in Proverbs that demonstrates part of what I mean. Wisdom speaks through parents instructing their son. "Do not forget my teaching, but keep my commands in your heart, for they will prolong your life many years and bring you peace and prosperity." Many people are happy to receive teaching, but they are not so happy when the teaching is about what God commanded. Yet God's commands are instructions about how to live in this world according to His design. If we want to experience a holistic life of well-being, we must, by His grace and power, do what He says.

There is a thread of moral command woven through Scripture that begins in Genesis and culminates in the teachings of Jesus and writings of the New Testament. It helps us understand how to live as God planned. If we pull at that thread, ignoring this part or that part of how God designed life to be lived, we limit the possibility of actualizing His full blessing.

There are those who misguidedly think that Jesus somehow lowered the moral standard through His teachings. In fact, He elevated it. He said that His followers should live more righteously than those who came before Him, including the teachers of the law. They said, for instance, not to commit adultery. His command, however, instructed that we were not to lust in our hearts. They said not to murder, but He said not to hate your brother. They said an eye for an eye, but He said to turn the other cheek and walk the extra mile. They said to love your neighbor, but He said love your enemy, too.

He finished the sermon where He taught these things by saying that the person who hears His teaching and puts His words into practice "is like a wise man who built his house on the rock. . . . But everyone who hears these words of mine and does not put them into practice is like a foolish man who built his house on sand." He was not kidding or merely suggesting. He really does expect us to keep His commands.

This is true of all of Scripture. We are to do what it teaches. God's Word is the instruction manual of how to live life the way God planned. And when we follow His commands, we receive the benefits of His other good intentions, such as His intention to bless us.

Thankfully, through His Spirit, Jesus helps us live life the way it was meant to be lived. We are told to take God and His Word seriously, and when we do, He will work in us to help us want to do and to do His good will.

Not one of us does all of this perfectly, of course, but this is the beauty of grace. "God saved you by his grace when you believed. . . . For we are God's masterpiece. He has created us anew in Christ Jesus, so we can do the good things he planned for us long ago."

By His grace, you are His masterpiece. With His help, you can live more and more the way He designed you to live, and you can receive more and more of the blessings He planned for you when He created you.

Do you ever try to fit God into the way you think life should be? Or are you happy to shape your life according to His design?

five

Church of the Rooster

Allow me to explain to you why I got angry at a place called the "Church of the Rooster." Sharon and I hosted a tour of the Holy Land and visited the Church of Saint Peter in Gallicantu that is just outside the wall surrounding ancient Jerusalem. This church is built on the site many archaeologists believe was the palace of Caiaphas the high priest, the guy who had Jesus arrested and put on trial. There is a dreadful dungeon underneath this church where it is believed Jesus was held on the evening of His trial before being turned over to the Roman governor Pilate.

This church takes its name from the Latin word *gallicatur*, loosely translated "rooster's crow." It is called the Church of the Rooster because the courtyard of the palace of Caiaphas is where Peter denied Jesus three times before the rooster crowed twice. Affixed to the roof of this church is a golden rooster that sits above a black cross. In the courtyard stands a large sculpture depicting Peter denying Jesus to a young woman as they warm themselves around a fire of coals with a Roman soldier standing ominously in the background.

Why did I get angry at the Church of the Rooster? Because this church memorializes the greatest mistake of Peter's life. When you think of Simon Peter, do you think of a rooster? I doubt it. Do you think failure? I hope not. Why? Because despite this one terribly dark night, Jesus forgave and redirected Simon Peter. And Peter went on to change the trajectory of human history and is revered as one of the greatest men who ever lived.

Let me be direct: You must not define your life by your mistakes nor let anyone else define your life by your mistakes. Human nature is inclined to focus on the thing that is done incorrectly rather than the thing that is done right. When it comes to God's desire to bless us, however, there is an extent to which neither matter—what you have done wrong or right—because His desire to bless us is sourced in Himself. Blessing flows from God's grace.

Grace. Grace. Grace. It is difficult to overemphasize God's grace. Grace is about God's desire and decision to be good to you. It is not about you doing enough good to earn His favor, nor is it about you doing enough bad to change God's mind. God's desire to bless you is what He wants. Yes, we can cooperate by aligning ourselves with His good intentions through actions such as faith and prayer and doing what He says, but we will not do these things perfectly. If we did, we would deserve to be blessed, and that would not be grace. God would not get to enjoy being a God of grace, which He does, in fact, greatly enjoy.

For most of us, however, the pressing issue is not pride in the good we do, because we are painfully aware of the good we do not do. We tend to memorialize our mistakes. We build monuments to our failures. Human beings have a bad news bias; we overlook one hundred good things done and remind ourselves constantly of one thing done wrong. Thankfully, though, the Gospel is all good news all the time. Despite your failures or successes, God is determined to bless you. This divine desire to bless you is rooted in His very nature.

One of the things I love about the story of Simon Peter and his signature failure was how Jesus knew he would fail, told him he would fail and promised to meet him on the other side of his failure to restore him to his purpose.

"You will all fall away," Jesus told them. . . . "But after I have risen, I will go ahead of you into Galilee." Peter declared, "Even if all fall away, I will not." "Truly I tell you," Jesus answered, "today—yes, tonight—before the rooster crows twice you yourself will disown me three times."

The region of Galilee was home for Peter and Jesus. Jesus was telling Peter that after his failure, He would be at home waiting for him. There is this great scene in the gospel of John in which, after His resurrection, Jesus cooked breakfast for Peter over a fire of coals on the shore of the Sea of Galilee. When Peter smelled that fire burning, his olfactory sense must have taken him back to that fire of coals in the courtyard of Caiaphas's palace—the scene of his failure. But at that breakfast, Jesus changed the narrative. He reconnected Peter to his destiny and redefined Peter's life as a success in progress regardless of the failures in his past.

I wish the Church of the Rooster would change its name. Maybe they could change it to the Church of Future Restoration, or the Church of the Heart of God to Bless Fallen People or the First Church of Grace. But even more, I pray that you will not define yourself by some mistake you have made or by your present shortcomings, because God does not define you in those ways.

Yes, He sees it all, including the places you have messed up, but He is not surprised, and He has not given up on you. He is just waiting for an opportunity to bring you back home to the Father—to a place where He can bless you. This gravitational God-force is always pulling you away from failure and toward a life that is blessed in every way.

I think authenticity is very important to this discussion. None of us is perfect, but we must be authentic. I once was invited by a generous friend to enjoy a baseball game in a suite at Yankee Stadium. While there, someone in Yankees management allowed us to handle one of Babe Ruth's bats. It was not perfect. It looked as if it had been used a number of times, and it was a little worse for the wear—but it was authentic.

Simon Peter was authentic. I love the raw humanity of his story. He clearly wanted to do the right things, but he struggled to do them. He was impulsive and brash, and yet he was tenderhearted and affectionate. He was gifted with deep spiritual insight, and yet he sometimes missed the deeper spiritual point entirely. He was self-sacrificing, yet self-seeking. In short, Peter was human. Jesus, however, loved him in all of his humanity and determined that He would work in Peter's life to make him everything God destined him to be. He did all of this despite the fact that he was often a study in contradictions. He was destined to be blessed and to bring blessing to the world, and that is exactly what he was and did.

In order for us to connect to God's desire to bless us, we must each bring our authentic selves to Him. "This is who I am. Here are my successes, and here are my failures." As the psalmist said, "For the honor of your name, O Lord, forgive my many, many sins." If you come to Him honestly, God will forgive your sins, reconcile you to Himself and reconnect you to your purpose.

God will not respond to your failures with a curse. That is not who He is. Many years after his insults and denials in the courtyard of Caiaphas's palace, the apostle Peter wrote to the Church, "Do not repay evil with evil or insult with insult. On the contrary, repay evil with blessing, because to this you were called so that you may inherit a blessing." This is what Peter experienced with Jesus. Even though he did curse, deny and fail at a place called the Church of the Rooster, his insult was returned with blessing that was inherited but not earned. This is called grace.

You may have failed, have probably failed in some way, but God is so gracious and so generous even in the face of insult and injury that you can expect to receive blessings unearned and yet given by God's grace.

Do you define yourself by failures and shortcomings, or as radically loved by a God of grace?

six

Prosperity Redefined

The more I study Scripture, the more convinced I become that God wants to prosper us, and the more convinced I become that prosperity has to do with much more than money and material things. The word in the New Testament translated *prosper* means "to help on one's way." The phrase *to prosper* in the Old Testament has to do with completing a successful venture. Prosperity is the abundance God supplies in every dimension of our lives as we move toward fulfilling our destiny. To prosper is to have more than we need in every circumstance as we fully become who we were made to be and fully live the life we were made to live.

The story of Joseph is a fascinating case study in prosperity. As a young person, Joseph had a God-inspired dream about his future. He then embarked—unwillingly—on a circuitous and extremely difficult journey toward the fulfillment of his dream. On this journey, Joseph was sold into slavery. Yet we are told that "the LORD was with Joseph so that he prospered, and he lived in the house of his Egyptian master. . . . The LORD gave him success in everything he did." On this journey, Joseph was thrown into prison. Yet we are told that "the LORD was with him; and whatever he did, the LORD made it prosper."

My guess is that neither slavery nor prison felt like prosperity to Joseph, but God was with him, developing him, using him, meeting his needs and working everything together for him as he was on his way to his destined place. It was not until the end of that journey—when Joseph's God-given dream came true—that he was able to articulate the truth that God had been good to him all along. He said that, despite the bad things his enemies had done against him, "God intended it for good to accomplish what is now being done."

In the end, Joseph became a man of great wealth and power. This was part of what prosperity was for him at that stage of his life. But God had prospered him every step of the way. Before his dream came true, he prospered. Before he had material wealth, he prospered. Before he had political power, he prospered. God was doing good to him while he was unjustly enslaved. God was doing good to him while he was unjustly imprisoned. And God was doing good to him while he was the second most powerful man in the world.

Sometimes we are blessed and unaware of blessing because God is doing good in us in ways that feel like He is not doing good to us at all. Remember that to be blessed is to be in harmonious relationship with God, who is doing good to us, in us and through us. Let's focus on the "in us" part of blessing for a few moments.

Donald Miller wrote, "A character who wants something and overcomes conflict to get it is the basic structure of a good story" and "the point of life is character transformation." This is a common theme among great writers and those who study story. A writer creates a character and then puts the character in situations where the character is transformed from one kind of person to another kind of person.

God, in His desire to truly bless us, is first and foremost interested in developing our character and transforming us from one kind of person to another kind of person— a better person who can live a better story. Specifically, those of us who follow Jesus are being transformed into His image. We are becoming more like Him—less like the fallen Adam and more like Jesus, the second Adam—so that we can live the life we were meant to live and do the things we were meant to do.

We know, however, from the teachings of Scripture and our own experience that our character is often forged in the furnace of difficulty. Sometimes then, when it seems as if God is not doing good to us, He actually is—more than we can possibly know. He is doing good in us. He is allowing the challenges of this fallen world—and our own fallenness—to place us in circumstances where our character is being transformed to be more like Jesus. And it doesn't get any better than that. Jesus is the most fully actualized person who has ever lived.

This much is certain: True prosperity is about so much more than accumulating money and possessions. I love the way Jesus reframed the concept of wealth when He said that if we have a proper attitude about money and practice good stewardship, we can be given "true riches." Financial wealth, if it is shared generously and if it is not chased, improperly obtained, trusted or allowed to become an idol, is generally viewed positively in Scripture.

But money does not equal true riches. True riches are the favor of God poured out into every area of our lives in a way that helps us develop fully as people. True riches lead us where God has called us to go. This favor is manifest in rich relationships, rich opportunities, rich sacrifices, rich mental health, rich spiritual lives and often financial blessings as long as material wealth serves the bigger picture of what it means to be truly rich.

Lady Wisdom captures this beautifully in her poem in Proverbs. She says, "With me are riches and honor, enduring wealth and prosperity. My fruit is better than fine gold; what I yield surpasses choice silver." She says that wise living will bring enduring wealth and prosperity, but that wisdom is better than any amount of money. If you are growing in your understanding of life as it was meant to be lived, then you may already be more prosperous than you ever imagined.

Please pay attention to the good God is doing in you, especially if you are facing difficult circumstances right now. He is prospering you. He is working to develop your character, and He is leading you to fulfill your God-inspired dreams. I predict that someday you will look back over the entirety of your life and clearly see that God has prospered you every step of your journey. You will see that you have been blessed in every way.

And if you are in a season now in which prosperity is being manifest in obvious and plentiful ways, enjoy every minute. Make certain the prosperity you are experiencing is rooted in a rich soul. I join with John the apostle in this simple prayer: "Beloved, I pray that you may prosper in all things and be in health, just as your soul prospers."

Are you able to identify a circumstance or season, past or present, in which you prospered but had been unaware of it until now?

seven

Meet the Gardener

S trategic thinkers tell us we should think from the future back—meaning that to most effectively think, decide and live now, we should have a picture in our minds of the future we desire and act today in a way that will help bring that preferred future to fruition. As believers, we should always have in our minds the eternal future we know God has planned, and we must allow that future reality to inform everything about our lives now.

I submit, however, that it may be even more important—from a scriptural perspective—to think from the past forward. Or more specifically, the beginning forward. The two are essentially the same, as the eternal future will reflect the very beginning. In the end, God will have what He began in Genesis. And somehow, the eternal future will be better because of everything that happens in the middle. We are in the middle now. This is the part of the plan God set in motion to end up with a forever that looks like what He had in mind when He created this world in the first place.

Our lives should be influenced every day by this reality. When we ask ourselves what God wants for us now, we should look to both the beginning and the end. In the beginning, human beings lived under God's blessing. This blessing showed up in a relationship with God so harmonious that they walked with Him in the Garden every day. This blessing showed up in their relationships—they were fully transparent with one another, unaffected by shame. This blessing showed up in their work—they worked so purposefully and joyfully that they did not even sweat. This blessing showed up in their health—they were not sick or in pain. This blessing showed up in their resources—they had everything they needed and more. This was life in all its fullness. This was the God-dreamed life.

This is what life will look like in the age to come. At the end of time as we know it, heaven will come down, renew our broken planet and form a new heaven and a new earth. There is a great line in J. R. R. Tolkien's *Lord of the Rings* when Samwise Gamgee, who had presumed that Gandalf was dead, realized that he was alive. He asks,

"Is everything sad going to come untrue?" The answer, of course, for those of us who believe in Jesus, is an unequivocal yes! Someday every sad thing will come untrue, and God will have in the end what He wanted in the beginning.

But what about now? What about those of us who are caught in the middle, where a lot of sad things are still true? First, we should live grounded in future hope.

> Our present sufferings are not worth comparing with the glory that will be revealed in us. . . . The whole creation has been groaning. . . . We ourselves . . . groan inwardly as we wait eagerly for . . . the redemption of our bodies. For in this hope we were saved. . . . In all things God works for the good of those who love him.

Future glory is reason for present hope.

Second, we should live believing that the future that manifests our genesis past will be reflected more and more in our day-to-day lives. A great biblical word is *regeneration*. When we believed in Jesus, we were born again, and when we were born again, we were regenerated and renewed by the Holy Spirit. *Regeneration*, in the original language of the New Testament, is a combination of the words *genesis* and *again*. To be born again—regenerated—is to experience genesis once again.

Do you remember that story in which Mary Magdalene was in the garden crying at the empty tomb? She turned and saw Jesus standing with her but mistook Him for the gardener. Well, He actually *was* the gardener. Not in that garden, but in the Garden of Eden. Jesus came to take us back and forward to the Garden of Eden.

Isaiah told us that Jesus, the Messiah, "will surely comfort Zion . . . ; he will make her deserts like Eden, her wastelands like the garden of the LORD." Jesus launched the ultimate reclamation project through His life, death, resurrection and exaltation. He entered this wasteland to regenerate it—to renew it. He is the Gardener, and He came to bring us genesis again. This. Matters. Now.

What would it look like for your life to reflect the Garden of Eden more and more? Your relationship with God? Your relationship with others? Your health? Your work life? Your financial life? I challenge you to look at some of the areas of your life that are more wilderness than garden and confess less wilderness and more garden.

One way that regeneration is understood is that to regenerate is to "re-create, especially in a better form or condition." I think the realities of the curse help us better appreciate present blessings. I believe that it is possible that we will enjoy the paradise of the new earth more than Adam and Eve enjoyed paradise lost. Perhaps it is only after evil has been experienced that good can be fully grasped. I am not saying the Fall was good, of course; it was not. I am saying that the redemption Jesus brings is so complete that everything will end up better than ever for those who now, by grace, choose good over evil.

Charles Colson eloquently wrote:

C. S. Lewis said that in every human story, as in divine history, there are two catastrophes. The first is utter ruin: the catastrophe of disintegration and undoing, the end of life as we know it, light extinguished in death's dark triumph. The crucifixion.

The second is the good catastrophe: the reintegrating and remaking, new hope rising out of the ashes—the good that would otherwise not be. The resurrection.

This is true in the great cosmic reality, and it is also true in the realities of our lives. The regeneration Jesus brings will re-create a better world in the age to come—somehow better for the catastrophe of the Fall—and His regenerative power in our lives now can make things better because of the sad things we have suffered.

One winter morning as I was walking through New York Penn Station, I heard a voice calling my name. I turned, and a young woman introduced herself to me. She was a successful Broadway actress on her way to an audition. She got out the information that she had been attending our church before she began to cry. She explained that she was pregnant, but there were problems with the baby. The baby, a girl, had been diagnosed with

Down syndrome, and ultrasounds had revealed two holes in her heart. She already loved this baby so much.

A few minutes later, we stood outside in the cold on Seventh Avenue, and over the sound of rush-hour traffic, I prayed a passionate prayer for her and her unborn daughter. I know in that season she had a lot of conflicting thoughts, but one must have been that this was a catastrophe. No one dreams of having a baby who has holes in her heart or who has a Down syndrome diagnosis.

But now, years later, that baby is a gorgeous little girl, miraculously healed from her heart condition, uniquely full of life and life-giving. This woman and her husband cannot imagine life without her, nor without her being exactly who she is, just as she is—a wonderfully healthy girl with Down syndrome. This is the good catastrophe. It is an outrageously good and beautiful blessing that would never have been if what had seemed to be a bad thing had not happened.

Sometimes the blessings we experience in this broken world are simply more precious because we are so aware that there are still some sad things that are true. In this way, our Eden blessings are better Eden blessings.

God's regenerative power can show up in any area of your life and make it better—especially when it appears as something bad. All the force of God and history are at work making things new. New like they were in the beginning, only better because of all we have been through. You have every reason to believe that everything in your life will keep becoming more and more the way God wants it to be. I encourage you to live as if you expect to be blessed—like God blessed His people in the beginning, but even better.

Do you have some area of your life that feels like wilderness but that you now believe will reflect Eden more and more?

SECTION 1 NOTES

▓ BLESS YOU: AN INTRODUCTION

God bless you was enshrined: Karen Harris, "'God Bless You' Sneeze Response: A Pope, a Plague, and a Proclamation," HistoryDaily.org, February 16, 2020, https://historydaily.org/god-bless-you-sneeze -response-pope-plague-proclamation.

"God blessed them": Genesis 1:28

"God's blessing on people involves": Tremper Longman III, *How to Read Genesis* (Downers Grove, IL: InterVarsity Press, 2005), 128.

"Blessing has to do with being in favor": John H. Walton, *The NIV Application Commentary: Genesis* (Grand Rapids, MI: Zondervan, 2001), 597.

It also has been defined as "multidimensional flourishing": Timothy Keller with Kathy Keller, *God's Wisdom for Navigating Life* (New York: Viking, 2017), 262.

▓ CHAPTER 1: ADAM SNEEZED

"For if, by the trespass of one man [Adam]": Romans 5:17 NIV1984

"Then God blessed Noah and his sons": Genesis 9:1

"I will make you into a great nation, and I will bless you": Genesis 12:2–3

"Abraham was now very old": Genesis 24:1

Guess what happened? "The Lord blessed him": Genesis 26:12

The Lord "blessed him there": Genesis 32:29

Scripture tells us that faith in Jesus: See Galatians 3:6–14

▓ CHAPTER 2: GOOD GOD

At the very beginning is "God blessed them": Genesis 1:28

"All behavior is based on a narrative": James Bryan Smith, *The Good and Beautiful Life* (Downers Grove, IL: InterVarsity Press, 2009), 24.

CHAPTER 3: ALIGN YOURSELF

"Has blessed us in the heavenly realms": Ephesians 1:3

Jesus taught us that when things are in proper order: Matthew 6:33

It is impossible to convey: Hebrews 11:6

Because he "believed the Lord": Genesis 15:6

And now God has chosen you: Galatians 3:14

God blessed Abraham in every way: Genesis 24:1

"So those who rely on faith are blessed": Galatians 3:9

When we pray, we are able to see things: Matthew 6:9–10

"The reason that you don't have what you want": James 4:2 NLT1996

"We can be confident that he will listen": 1 John 5:14–15 NLT1996

"Fulfill every good purpose of yours": 2 Thessalonians 1:11 NIV1984

CHAPTER 4: LIVE A MASTERPIECE

This is part of the message of Lady Wisdom: For an expansive teaching on this thought, see my message series on Proverbs, *Ancient Wisdom: Learn the Secrets to a Fulfilling Life*, available at www.terryasmith.com/wisdom. See also my message series *Rich Relationships: Invest in Your Marriage, Family, and Friendships* at www.terryasmith.com/relationships.

"I was the architect at his side": Proverbs 8:30–31 NLT

"Do not forget my teaching": Proverbs 3:1–2

"Is like a wise man who built": Matthew 7:24–27

"God saved you by his grace when you believed": Ephesians 2:8–10 NLT

CHAPTER 5: CHURCH OF THE ROOSTER

"You will all fall away": Mark 14:27–30

"For the honor of your name": Psalm 25:11 NLT

"Do not repay evil with evil": 1 Peter 3:9

■ CHAPTER 6: PROSPERITY REDEFINED

"To help on one's way": W. E. Vine, Merrill F. Unger, and William White Jr., *Vine's Complete Expository Dictionary* (Nashville: Thomas Nelson, 1985), 495.

The phrase *to prosper* in the Old Testament: Vine, Unger, and White, *Vine's Complete Expository Dictionary*, 191.

"The Lord was with Joseph": Genesis 39:2–4

"The Lord was with him": Genesis 39:23 NKJV

"God intended it for good": Genesis 50:19–21

"The point of life is character transformation": Donald Miller, *A Million Miles in a Thousand Years* (Nashville: Thomas Nelson, 2011, First Edition), 48, 68.

"With me are riches": Proverbs 8:18–19

"Beloved, I pray that you may prosper in all things and be in health, just as your soul prospers": 3 John 1:2 NKJV

■ CHAPTER 7: MEET THE GARDENER

"Is everything sad going to come untrue?": J. R. R. Tolkien, *The Lord of the Rings* (Boston: Houghton Mifflin, 1938), 951.

"For in this hope we were saved": Romans 8:18–28

When we believed in Jesus, we were born again: Titus 3:4–5

"Will surely comfort Zion": Isaiah 51:3

"Re-create, especially in a better form": "Regenerate," Dictionary.com, 2022, https://www.dictionary.com/browse/regenerate.

"C. S. Lewis said that in every human story": Charles Colson and Ellen Vaughn, *Being the Body: A New Call for the Church to Be Light in the Darkness* (Nashville: Thomas Nelson, 2003), 3.

PURPOSE

eight

Blessing and Purpose

Here is one of the most consequential truths I have ever learned, breathtaking in both its simplicity and importance: God's blessing in our lives is inextricably linked to fulfilling our purpose.

When God first interacted with the human beings He created, He blessed them. In the same breath—literally the same sentence—He delineated their purpose. "So God created human beings in his own image. . . . Then God blessed them and said, 'Be fruitful and multiply. Fill the earth and govern it.'" These people who were created in God's image were to multiply the God-image throughout the earth. They were to take what they had in the Garden of Eden—God's presence, unashamed relationships, abundance, beauty and more—and fill the earth with it. They were to establish God's rule everywhere on this planet and govern the created world under His authority. In short, they were to both partner with God in intimate relationship and partner with Him to do His work. Blessing was not just about the good God wanted to do to them and in them, but blessing was also the good He wanted to do with them and through them.

You may, understandably, feel radically distant from the Creation narrative and what Scripture tells us that God wanted us to know about His first interaction with people. But you shouldn't. God has not changed His mind about His desire to bless the people He made, nor has He changed His mind about what He fundamentally made people to do. He wants you to join Him in doing good in this world. He wants to bless the world through you.

When we come into relationship with God through Jesus, we should not only think about reconciliation with God, but we should also think about how we were restored to our God-given purpose. We are now able to do what we were created for. Fulfillment lives here. "God saved you by his grace when you believed. . . . For we are God's masterpiece. He has created us anew in Christ Jesus, so we can do the good things he planned for us long ago." You were saved to do what you were made to do.

On August 7, 1974, Philippe Petit, a young Frenchman, illegally rigged a wire between the Twin Towers that were then standing in lower Manhattan. The towers stood nearly 1,400 feet high and 140 feet apart. At that height, there was ever-present wind and mist, and a constant but imperceptible give and movement between the Towers. But Petit wanted to walk on the wire.

So after years of planning, he and some co-conspirators somehow eluded security and fastened one end of the wire to each tower. Then, out onto the wire he went. And Philippe did not just walk on the wire . . . he danced on the wire for nearly an hour. He danced on the wire! The video of this event shows that as he danced, he had a look of sheer joy on his face. Later, after he was arrested, jailed—given a psychological evaluation!—and then released, he said he had felt such pleasure because he was doing "what I was made to do." I cannot judge whether he was actually made to do that, but I get it. When you do what you were made to do, even if it seems crazy, you live in a perpetual joy-filled condition called *blessed*.

On one hand, we were all made to do the same thing—to be in relationship with God and to partner with Him to do His work. Yet within that common purpose, we each have a unique role to play. I submit that you cannot fully experience God's blessing unless you are fulfilling your specific purpose in alignment with what all of us are purposed for. Let's explore three big words in the Genesis narrative that can help us get an understanding of God's purpose for our lives: create, image and sin.

First, the word *create* in the original language had to do with "bringing heaven and earth into existence ... the assignment of roles and functions" and is connected to "the fixing of destinies." Part of what happened when God created was that He assigned a purpose to everything and every being. He had a reason for creating everything and everyone. You have a purpose. All of us were made to worship God and to do His work. But within that larger purpose, we each have an assigned role—or roles—to play. This assigned role is manifest in how we relate with God and others through our vocations, by using our gifts to serve in and from the Church and in other ways. You will experience the deep satisfaction of destiny fulfillment when you play your assigned role.

Second, we were created in God's *image*. This means in part that we reflect and represent God in this world. We are image bearers. God's image in human beings was damaged because of human choices. Through Jesus, however, the God-image is being repaired. As we grow in our relationship with Jesus, we are "being transformed into his image with ever-increasing glory." We must focus on our relationship with Jesus and know that as we do, we will become more like Him and more capable of representing God in this world.

Third, we need to talk about *sin*. The word most commonly translated as *sin* in the New Testament means "missing the mark." Imagine your life as an arrow in a bow that is aimed by God at the bull's-eye of a target. That bull's-eye is your destiny. God aims you, releases you and allows you to choose whether you will hit the target. To miss the mark is to miss what God made you to be and do with your life. We must live out our God-designed purpose, and the good news is that we can. And if we are presently not living out our purpose, it is never too late to confess our sin, turn from our sin, turn to God and let Him reconnect us to the purpose and the blessing He wants to give.

You can discover your purpose and live the life God created you to live. Ask Him to show you your assigned role and to give you the opportunities and power to do the good work He planned for you long ago. He wants to bless you and bless the world around you through you. This could get very exciting!

Do you know your purpose? Are you living on purpose?

nine

Invitation to Adventure

❧

I love the scene in the opening pages of *The Hobbit* where Gandalf visits the well-to-do and quite comfortable Bilbo Baggins. He challenges him to join him "in an adventure that I am arranging." Bilbo quickly replies, "We are plain quiet folk and have no use for adventures. Nasty disturbing uncomfortable things! Make you late for dinner!" Bilbo's mother, however, was a Took, and "once in a while members of the Took-clan would go and have adventures." In a moment of clarity "something Tookish woke up inside him, and he wished to go and see the great mountains, and hear the pine-trees and the waterfalls, and explore the caves, and wear a sword instead of a walking-stick." So Bilbo said yes. He went, and in the fantastic world of *The Lord of the Rings*, he was used mightily to advance good and defeat evil. It was a great adventure.

I am moved by the idea that there was something in Bilbo's Tookish DNA that woke up to Gandalf's call. I believe, in a very real-world sense, there is something Adamic in us that wants to respond to God's call, to reconnect us to what the first human beings experienced when God blessed them and invited them to join Him in His ongoing creative activity on this planet. What a call. What an adventure.

Genesis tells us that God put Adam in Eden to "work it and take care of it." This is fundamental to our purpose. God planted the Garden of Eden, but Adam was purposed to work on what God worked on and to care about what God cared about. Moreover, whereas Eden was lush, the rest of the earth was barren, and Adam and Eve were to spread the beauty of the Garden and the rule of God to the entire earth. They were not to just hang out in Eden and live nice, comfortable lives; they were blessed to bless the world. This is what they were made for. And this is in our DNA.

Life becomes meaningful when we wake up to who we were made to be and what we were made to do. This is why there is nothing as fulfilling as being in intimate relationship with God and doing work that reflects what He cares about. Blessing is woven through every part of engaging in our God-designed purpose.

Let's focus on saying yes to God's call. Perhaps you already have. If so, you are already tasting the joy of joining God in His work. Perhaps, though, you are not sure what God is calling you to do. I assure you that you will come alive to His call if you cultivate your spiritual life, pay attention to the needs in the world around you, are aware of your passions, discover the gifts that are in you and work to develop those gifts into skills. We will explore this in more detail in chapter 10, but for now, decide to say yes to whatever God calls you to do.

Maybe God is calling you to start a new business, become a foster parent, go back to school or step out in faith and sacrifice to serve in some ministry. Say yes to whatever He is calling you to, even if it disrupts your nice, comfortable life. Blessing is found in joining God in His great adventure.

Here is a pivotal moment in human history. God said to Abraham:

> "Go from your country, your people and your father's household to the land I will show you. . . . I will bless you . . . and you will be a blessing. . . . All peoples on the earth will be blessed through you." So Abram went, as the Lord had told him.

Tremper Longman III wrote, "This is almost like a second creation account. . . . Now that the divine-human relationship had been broken (God) speaks again to Abraham in order to create a new people on whom he will place his blessing." I think when God called Abraham, something Adamic woke up in him. God wanted to do through Abraham what He had planned to do in the beginning, and He hoped to show all of us what it looks like to say yes to His call.

When Abraham was called to go, he lived in a sophisticated and desirable city named Ur. He was called to go to a yet unnamed place that God would show him. He was asked to go before he even knew exactly where to go. Where he ended up going was not nearly as geographically desirable as the place that he left, but God made it a place of immense blessing.

When we read at the end of Abraham's life that he was "blessed in every way," we must remember that earlier in his life, Abraham had said yes to God's call. This is not an "Abraham lived a nice little life" blessing. This was "Abraham risked everything to fulfill his God-given purpose" blessing. Blessing is inextricably linked to fulfilling God's purposes in our lives.

Here is a crazy story. It is a story that has shaped everything in my life. One day when I was in seventh grade, I was playing basketball on the driveway of the idyllic white-picket-fence home our family lived in, in a suburb of Indianapolis. My dad, who had just arrived home from work, called me to come into the house. I went in and saw he had called the rest of the family, too—my mom and younger sister.

His voice broke as he told us that while he had been driving that day, God had spoken to him—not in an audible voice, but unmistakable nonetheless—and that God had called him into vocational ministry. He said that God's presence was so strong that he had to stop on the side of the road to keep from wrecking the car. Sitting in that car, my dad simply said yes.

Everything changed forever for our family in that moment. Dad was a successful businessman, and we had lived a very comfortable life. A lot of people would say that we had been living the American dream. But it was not what God had dreamed for us. Something woke up that day in my dad and somehow, by God's grace, something woke up in the rest of our family.

After a few years of preparation, my parents sold virtually everything we owned, and we embarked as a family on an adventure that has taken us places none of us ever would have imagined. It was wonderfully disruptive. When my dad said yes to that call—when he risked everything to fulfill his God-destined purpose—it opened a window in heaven through which blessing has been poured out on each of us in ways I cannot begin to comprehend or explain. And my dad's yes taught me to say yes when God calls me to do crazy things, too. What adventure! What blessing!

Your story does not need to be so dramatic. But please, however, whenever and to whatever God calls you, say yes. Your yes to God's call might disrupt your nice, comfortable life, but I promise it will make it more and better than you ever dreamed.

What adventure is God calling you to?

ten

Indispensable You

Y ou were made to play an essential role in this world. This world cannot be all it was meant to be without you. I know there is another perspective that argues we are each just one of 125 billion people who have lived on this planet, that when we die the world will go on fine without us and that none of us are indispensable. Yet there is ample evidence in Scripture that God placed each of us here at this time and place to play a necessary role in His unfolding plan to bless the world. God's words to Jeremiah ring in my ear: "Before I formed you in the womb I knew you, before you were born I set you apart; I appointed you."

I was deeply moved when George W. Bush wrote that his parents' lives were forever changed when their three-year-old daughter, Robin, died in 1953. Though they went on from that loss to achieve the heights of success, including his dad being elected president of the United States, and though they had four other children who have lived full lives, including one becoming a United States president as well, they still had an un-fillable hole in their hearts. George H. W. and Barbara Bush led wonderful lives, but they were never the same after they lost their daughter. Robin was irreplaceable.

Allow me to tell you something that should be obvious but often is not: You have a place in the heart of God that can only be filled with you. I do not know how He keeps track of all His kids, but He does. Jesus said, "Are not five sparrows sold for two pennies? Yet not one of them is forgotten by God. . . . Don't be afraid; you are worth more than many sparrows."

You have an indispensable role to play in God's life and His world, a role that can only be played by you. This does not mean that God cannot get on without you. He can. But He wants *you*! This does not mean that the world cannot get on without you. We can. But we need *you*!

I wonder what would happen if we each saw our lives through the lens of indispensability—if we each knew how much we are wanted and needed. I am the pastor of a church that someday will move on without me. I know this. Yet I believe I must see myself as placed in this position for this time, conduct myself as though I have an essential role to play and work as if what I do is indispensable for the success of this church. This is not ego gratification. This is accepting responsibility, believing God knew me before I was born, set me apart and appointed me to be and do what He made me to be and do.

We must each live out our indispensability. The apostle Paul challenged us like this: "I beg you to live in a way that is worthy of the people God has chosen to be his own." I want you to experience the unparalleled blessing that comes when you live like you are the person God destined you to be.

You can know the role you were destined to play. I wrote at some length in my book *The Hospitable Leader* about a concept that has helped a lot of people discover their God appointed role. It is called Area of Destiny. Your Area of Destiny is what God made your life to be about. It is a life-organizing principle. It defines the boundaries and possibilities of your life. It is the context in which you can play your indispensable role and enjoy the sweet spot of blessing fully known only when you do.

Area of Destiny is discovered in the intersect of Mission (What is God doing and where are you needed?)— Passion (What good things do you love to do? What makes you come alive?)—and Gifts (What talents have you been given, and what action needs to be taken to turn those gifts into skills?) Mission—Passion—Gifts. Each should be explored as part of a spiritual quest focused on

God and His plan for our lives. We can know what God had in mind when He made us, what He "destined for our glory before time began." This plan is so marvelous it can only be "revealed to us by his Spirit. The Spirit searches all things, even the deep things of God." God will not give you a detailed, day-by-day agenda, but He will give you a profound sense of what He made your life to be about. He will work in you and through you to help you play the role that you were uniquely cast to play.

Abraham and Ruby Thomas immigrated from India to the United States in 1992. When I met them soon after, I was the young pastor of a new church—the church I still serve today. Both Abe and Ruby were well on their way to finishing their training to become medical doctors. They had one young son and another on the way. They quickly became active members of the church and good friends to me and my wife, Sharon. As they finished their medical residencies, they were deluged with opportunities to move to other areas of the United States to join successful medical practices and begin their new lives in places far less complicated than the northern New Jersey/ New York City metro area.

It became apparent, much to my disappointment, that they had, understandably, decided to leave. Then one day I got a call from Abe that I remember well. I thought he had called to tell me where they had decided to move, and I was sad to take the call.

He said, however, "Ruby and I have been doing a lot of praying and talking about our future, and we have decided to stay here. We feel called to raise our family here, to build our medical practices here and to center our lives around helping you and the other leaders grow this church. We believe this area needs this church and that we have a role to play here."

That was nearly thirty years ago. As I write this, they have done exactly what they felt God called them to do. They have raised two amazing sons to adulthood, built successful medical careers and helped grow our church to have a powerful impact on this region. They have influenced countless people in ways that will only be fully realized in the age to come. Everything in their lives became about what they believed God made their lives to be about. They have played indispensable roles in their Area of Destiny, and as a consequence, they and so many others have experienced immeasurable blessing.

I encourage you to explore your unique place in this world, to ask questions about mission, passion and gifts, and most of all, to ask God to bring all of this together by His Spirit to reveal what is in His mind for you. He has astounding plans for you!

Are you living out your indispensability?

eleven

Someday Morning

❦

There is an astonishing moment in antiquity when God reveals to David, the second king of Israel, marvelous plans for David's future and the future of his family. God tells David that his son will sit on his throne forever. This prophecy was fulfilled in Jesus, Son of David, to whom was given "the holy and sure blessings promised to David." David responds to these promised blessings with delighted wonderment. He can hardly believe that God has promised him—him of all people!—such a wonderful future. Yet he does believe. Here is part of David's response to God's blessing:

"Who am I . . . that you have brought me this far? . . . You speak as though I were someone very great, O Lord

God! . . . You know what your servant is really like. . . .
And you have promised these good things. . . . it has
pleased you to bless the house of your servant, so that it
will continue forever before you. For when you grant a
blessing, O Lord, it is an eternal blessing!"

Two things occur to me as I read David's reaction to
God's astounding promises. First, I hope as you are learn-
ing more about God's promise to bless you that you, too,
are overwhelmed with joy and faith. It may seem too good
to be true, but God does things that are too good to be
true all the time.

Second, I am struck by how God's past blessings, present blessings and promised blessings for David's future
were connected to the fact that David had done and was
doing what God purposed him to do. At the beginning
of the David story, we are told God chose him because
David was a person who would do what He called him
to do. "I have found David . . . a man after my own heart;
he will do everything I want him to do." We must note
again that God's blessings in a person's life are inextricably
linked to that person fulfilling God's purposes.

Sometimes I hear people talk about how God chose
David in a way that I think misses the point. They talk
about how David had a heart after God. They focus on
his passionate love for God, which is incredibly important
and wonderful, of course; however, when God looked at

David, He did not just see a nice guy who loved Him. He saw someone who would do what He wanted Him to do. "David . . . is the kind of person who pleases me most! He does everything I want him to do." God had an indispensable role for David to play, and He knew David would play it. When God looks in your heart, does He see a person who is ready to do whatever God wants you to do?

One of the first times we encounter David, we get a sense of why God found David so choosable and so blessable. When David was a young man, already secretly anointed to be king yet years from ascending the throne, he was sent by his father to check on his older brothers, who were soldiers in Israel's army. The Israelites had set up a battle line on a hill against their most notorious enemy, the Philistines, who occupied a hill opposite them. Goliath, a giant of a man who stood nearly nine and a half feet tall and who was skilled in hand-to-hand combat, came every day into the valley between these two armies trying to get an Israelite—any Israelite—to fight him. He defied God and Israel's army. Not one man was willing to take him on. Except David. He assertively went to Israel's King Saul and insisted on being awarded the opportunity to represent the demoralized army and fight Goliath.

My favorite part of the story is the verbiage David used to convince Saul that he could handle Goliath. He told Saul that when he was shepherding his family's flocks and a lion or bear came to carry off a sheep, he "went after it, struck it and rescued the sheep." When the lion or bear turned to attack him, David said, "I seized it by its hair, struck it and killed it." This speech won him permission to face Goliath. And when he did, "David ran quickly toward the battle line to meet him." The rest is history.

When God chose David, He did not just see a handsome, uber-talented, shepherd, musician and warrior who loved God with all of his heart, which of course, He did. He also saw someone who would look at an opportunity and be the guy who *seized it*, who would see a challenge and be the one who *went after it* and who would face a threat and be the person who *ran quickly* to defeat it.

This mentality is evident throughout David's life. Even on his deathbed he orchestrated events to make certain that Solomon, his chosen heir, would sit on his throne even though powerful enemies were plotting against them. He charged Solomon to "be strong, act like a man," and David bowed down "in worship on his bed."

I am tremendously inspired by David's go-after-it attitude. I am also strangely warmed by the reality that David was human. Though he did what God called him to do, he made plenty of mistakes along the way, even some famously egregious ones. Yet when confronted with his shortcomings and sins, he was honest and repentant. "Have mercy on me, O God. . . . Cleanse me from my sin. For I know my transgressions. . . . Create in me a pure heart." One reason David was overwhelmed when God continued to grant and promise "rich. . . . unending blessings" stretching far into the future, is captured in these simple words: "You know what your servant is really like."

You may be fully engaged in your Area of Destiny doing exactly what God called you to do. I believe I am. If you are like me, however, you are also painfully aware of your weaknesses and the mistakes you have made. You are acutely cognizant that you are not perfectly doing everything you are meant to do. We need to keep showing up every day, to go after it and always be honest with God, ourselves and others about our need for mercy and grace.

Or perhaps you are not only aware of your weaknesses and mistakes, but you also do not feel as if you are fully engaged in what you were made to do. It is never too late to report for your destiny and say to God, "I will do whatever You want me to do."

Some time ago I received an eloquent email from a woman in my congregation. I had been challenging the good folks I preach to Sunday after Sunday to say yes to God's call. I reminded them that when they did, they would be blessed beyond their wildest imagination. This woman told me she kept saying, "Someday. Someday when I know exactly what to do. Someday when I feel more qualified. Someday when everything is just right."

She had recently lost a sister due to complications from alcoholism. Her grief was one of her "someday" excuses.

On the morning she wrote me, she had received an invitation to get involved in a home for women who were recovering from alcoholism and other substance abuse issues. She had been asking God to help with grief, but she realized that God might be answering her prayer by inviting her to serve women who were struggling with the issues that had ended her sister's life. She wrote that it was as if God said, "If you help Me, I'll help you. I can't give you your sister back, but I can give you the opportunity to help eight other women like her. Get off the couch and say yes. Because it's Someday Morning, and we need to get to work."

If you have been saying *someday*, I encourage you to accept God's invitation. As David did, do whatever He asks you to do. It is Someday Morning, and it is time to get to work.

Are you ready to say yes to God's call and receive unending blessings?

twelve

Risk and Reward

I s it possible to partner with God in such a way that He multiplies what we have and blesses us with more so that we can enjoy the life we have been given and do more good in this world? Yes. Absolutely yes!

The desire to be productive, to increase, to become many or to become much was woven into the fabric of humanity in the very beginning. This is shown in the purpose statement God gave the first man and woman when He blessed them. They were to reproduce who they were and to fill the earth with their progeny. They were to take what they had cultivated and produced in the Garden and spread it to the world. Their blessing from God was directly connected to fulfilling this mandate to partner with Him to make more of what they had been given.

I love the words of the apostle Paul in his letter to the Corinthians when he said that the number of seeds they would sow through giving would determine the size of their harvest. Their harvest was the amount of blessing they would receive to meet their own needs and the increase they would receive in their capacity to do good to others.

> Remember this saying, "A few seeds make a small harvest, but a lot of seeds make a big harvest." Each of you must make up your own mind about how much to give. . . . God can bless you with everything you need, and you will always have more than enough to do all kinds of good things for others.

God will multiply what you have when you invest in what He cares about and is working on. And the more you invest, the more He multiplies, and the more He multiplies, the more you experience good and expand your ability to do good to others. "God is able to bless you abundantly, so that in all things at all times, having all that you need, you will abound in every good work."

When you do what you were made to do, when you invest your time, talent and treasure to partner with God in what He is doing in your world, it has a multiplicative effect. God takes little and makes it more. God does not just bless us as we fulfill our purpose; He multiplies blessings the more we fulfill our purpose.

To some extent, the blessing question is how much blessing do you want? To which I enthusiastically respond, "Why wouldn't we want more?" This is not selfish. God multiplies blessings so that we can do greater good. I propose that selfishness is not wanting more blessings. God wants to bless you and this—fulfilling your God-given purpose and excelling in good works—is why. I encourage you to want more! This is an essential part of practicing responsible life stewardship.

Life stewardship begins with acknowledging God as the owner of all we are and have, and then living as stewards of God's property. This is bigger than just caring for what we have. It is also about making more of it for God's sake. Good stewards are managers and investors.

This is demonstrated beautifully in the parable Jesus told about a prince who called together several servants before he left his land to be crowned king. He gave each of them a generous amount of money to invest while he was gone. When he returned, he called his servants back together to find out how much they had earned.

The first guy had earned a thousand percent return. The king exclaimed, "Since you have shown that you can be trusted with a small amount, you will be given ten cities to rule." That is a lot of opportunity to do good! The second guy brought a return of five hundred percent, and his faithfulness with little was multiplied into authority over five cities.

The third guy just returned the initial investment. He thought it was enough to just take care of what he had been given. To which the king reacted:

> "Why didn't you put my money in the bank? On my return, I could have had the money together with interest." Then he said to some other servants standing there, "Take the money away from him and give it to the servant who earned it ten times as much." But they said, "Sir, he already has ten times as much!" The king replied, "Those who have something will be given more. But everything will be taken away from those who don't have anything."

God expects us to make more of what we have been given, and He gives us more blessing and more opportunity to do good when we do. The rewards for playing it safe are minimal at best, dangerous at worst. God richly rewards people who dream big and pray big and take big risks to play the role they were made for. *The Message* records that Jesus said, "That's what I mean: Risk your life and get more than you ever dreamed of. Play it safe and end up holding the bag."

Are you willing to take whatever risk is necessary for whatever you sense God is calling you to do? Maybe you are feeling moved to start a new business that honors God and serves people in a for-profit context, or to launch a nonprofit that meets some societal need, or to go back to school to prepare to fully engage in your Area of Destiny, or to write a really large check—or checks—that will make a significant impact in moving the mission forward in your local church. May I suggest that the greatest risk is not doing what you are being called to do? When you risk for your King and His Kingdom, He will advance you, promote you and increase you. He will give you more authority, more responsibility and more ability to do good. He will multiply blessings as you more fully engage in the things you were made for.

Risk, by definition, means that there is a possibility of loss. When we take risks in obedience to God, however, we are playing with house money. He is the owner of all that we are and have, and we can only risk what He has given us. When we invest to advance God's Kingdom and it appears as if we have suffered loss, we must remember that there is more going on than we can see. As Jesus said:

> "I assure you that everyone who has given up house or brothers or sisters or mother or father or children or property, for my sake and for the Good News, will receive now in return a hundred times as many houses, brothers, sisters, mothers, children, and property—along with persecution. And in the world to come that person will have eternal life."

God is in the multiplication business. He has been since the beginning, and He will be in the age to come. If you live in full-throated obedience to whatever God asks you to do, He will multiply blessings in your life now and forever. You simply cannot lose.

What are you willing to risk to say yes to God's call?

thirteen

Resistance Training

It was a glorious summer day when I tromped through waist-high weeds in the middle of an abandoned eight-acre property on a four-lane avenue just thirteen miles from Times Square. I told a dubious staff pastor who was with me that I believed God had called our congregation to acquire this property and build a Worship and Mission Center. It was unkempt, overgrown and forgotten land.

I said, "Where we are walking right now is where I envision people will someday sit in a beautiful building and worship together. I know it seems way out of our reach—impossible, even—but I believe this is what God is asking us to do. Let's stand here now and pray a prayer of faith together." It was a glorious winter day ten years later when we worshiped in that Worship and Mission Center for the first time.

Between those two glorious days, however, I suffered through many inglorious ones. Ten long years of complicated, multiparty negotiations, of zoning, planning and Township Council meetings, of not-in-my-backyard neighbors, of unscrupulous opponents who spread terrible lies about me and our church in an attempt to stop the project altogether, of bond programs, capital campaigns and loans, of blasting and removing one million dollars of rock just to prepare the site, of construction setbacks, stoppages and construction again, of building inspections and certificates of occupancy, and of—if you have seen my picture—a considerable loss of hair. In short, between vision conception and vision realization we faced a whole lot of resistance.

To actualize any God-inspired calling we must overcome conflict. In my experience, the bigger the God-given dream, the more conflict we must overcome to see the dream come true. Steven Pressfield wrote:

> Most of us have two lives. The life we live and the unlived life within us. Between the two stands Resistance. . . . You must declare Resistance evil, for it prevents us from achieving the life God intended when He endowed each of us with our own unique genius.

God will use this evil for good, however. He exploits resistance to make us better and to build our character. Character is developed when we fight for the things to which we have been called. Character provides the inner infrastructure needed to fully embrace the life God dreams for us. It is used to give birth to the dreams He has conceived in us.

Exercise physiologists tell us that resistance training is necessary to enjoy optimal levels of health and longevity. It is not enough only to practice aerobic exercise. We must challenge our muscles and other physical systems with significant resistance to increase our strength and vitality, especially as we age. I am reminded of a guy who said that he does not like to lift weights. When asked why, he answered, "Because they are heavy." But, of course, heavy is the point. We need resistance to grow stronger and to enhance holistic health.

When this principle is applied to the more important things in life, it gives us reason to celebrate resistance. The apostle James wrote in his letter to first-century believers:

> Dear brothers and sisters, when troubles of any kind come your way, consider it an opportunity for great joy. For you know that when your faith is tested, your endurance has a chance to grow. So let it grow, for when your endurance is fully developed, you will be perfect and complete, needing nothing.

If you are not facing some difficulty as you say yes to fulfilling your purpose, you are probably not growing stronger in character. When resistance is heavy, you have a reason for great joy.

Those inglorious days between call and fulfillment, dream and actualization, promise and provision are actually glorious in their own way. Part of what it means to be blessed is to be called to join God on a great adventure. Adventures are wild, dangerous things that are full of risk and heart-thumping excitement. Tim Ferriss wrote that the opposite of happiness is not sadness, but rather, "the opposite of happiness is . . . boredom." Fulfilling our purpose will not be boring, but it will not be easy, either. That is okay. We all need some resistance training.

It is revealing that God set up the potential for conflict in the very beginning. God wanted people to say yes to blessing and purpose even when facing evil. Those first human beings failed and opened the floodgates of resistance. For us to get back to the way things should be, we also must say yes to blessing and to the fulfillment of our purpose even in the face of evil.

There are three primary sources of resistance. First, our own sinful nature, that part of us that wants to operate independently of God. We must surrender constantly to our new nature, the divine nature, to resist our sinful nature.

Second, the world, or the way things are in this world as a result of the Fall. We can change the way things are as we work with God to bring His rule and shalom, where everything is more and more the way it was meant to be.

Third, the evil one. Ultimately, evil is not a concept but a person. The Bible teaches us that if we will submit to God and resist the evil one, he "will run from you." We have power to resist the resistance through the Word of God, the victory of Jesus over sin and death, prayer, praise and an array of other spiritual weaponry and impenetrable spiritual armor. We will face resistance and must know that we can fight it, defeat it and be better because we did.

Many years ago, Sharon and I took our children to the American Museum of Natural History. I was struck by an exhibit featuring a composite of the dodo bird. It could not display an exact replica, because there are no more in existence, and there have not been any for a long time. The dodo lived on islands near Africa where they had no enemies. They did not develop wings sufficient to fly, nor claws and beaks sharp enough to fight. They grew big, fat bodies that were insufficient for anything more than lazy existence. Now they are extinct. Why? Because people came to occupy these islands, and they brought with them predatory animals who killed and ate the defenseless dodos—until there were no dodos at all.

You probably know what I am about to say. It is an obvious and silly statement, but here it is nonetheless: Do not be a dodo. Do not be satisfied with a life of comfort and ease that does not have risks. Fulfilling our purpose gives us something to fight for. That is part of God's blessing. Embrace the conflict between good and evil. He is preparing you for more now and forever.

Thankfully, we are not in this alone. The best part of the adventure, of facing the resistance, is that we are in partnership with God. We are in this with Him. I like to define prayer as "communication between a person and God about who they are, and what they are thinking and doing together." God allows us to face conflict, but He does not intend that we face it alone. He wants us to be in harmonious relationship with Him, to walk and talk with Him, to depend on Him, to enjoy Him and to be victorious through Him. This is about what we are doing together.

I encourage you to confess this now. Expect to be blessed, especially as you face all kinds of challenges. "If God is for us, who can be against us? . . . In all these things we are more than conquerors through him who loved us."

Do you see resistance as an opportunity for joy?

fourteen

No Sweat

t is impossible to overstate how gratifying it is to work hard in alignment with our purpose and with the energy of God's blessing.

It is not uncommon to hear experts extol the phenomenon of *flow*. Flow is what people experience when they perform a task so aligned with their abilities and passions that they seemingly expend little effort and experience great pleasure, regardless of the level of difficulty. This might be a gifted athlete playing a great game, or an artist enraptured as they paint, or a carpenter caught up in enjoyment of their work and losing all sense of time. As wonderful as this kind of flow is, I submit that there is a supernatural flow far beyond any of this.

When God is present in our lives and gives us His favor, we do what we do with His energy, and we experience a beyond-normal dimension of joy. Paul wrote to the Colossians, "This is my work and I can do it only because Christ's mighty energy is at work within me." This is better than flow. This is blessing.

This does not mean that hard work is not hard work. Hard work is celebrated in Scripture. It is just that when we are working in partnership with God, we somehow find rest in our work despite how challenging that work may be. Jesus invites us to, "Take my yoke upon you and learn from me . . . and you will find rest for your souls. For my yoke is easy and my burden is light."

A yoke was a wooden frame used to join two animals together—usually oxen—to pull a heavy load. Jesus wants us to be yoked with Him, to walk with Him and to work with Him, but He lets us know that He will exert His power to help pull the load. When we say yes to His call, we do, in fact, risk, sacrifice and face resistance. This can be hard, and yet paradoxically, it can be easy at the same time.

Eugene Peterson translates Jesus' words eloquently. "Walk with me and work with me—watch how I do it. Learn the unforced rhythms of grace. . . . Keep company with me and you'll learn to live freely and lightly." This is the Gospel. This is grace. If you trust Jesus to walk with you and work with you, you will flourish in the depths of your soul.

I find it helpful to think about it this way: Part of the blessing in the beginning was sweatless work. When Adam worked in the Garden, he evidently did not sweat, at least not in the same way he sweat after the Fall. Part of the curse was, "By the sweat of your brow you will eat your food until you return to the ground." Adam had undoubtedly worked hard in Eden, but it was a different kind of work because it was done in perfect harmony with God, purposed by God and blessed by God. A consequence of his choice was that his wilderness work would be sweaty work. He was going to have to sweat his way to accomplish what had previously come so easily.

I find it fascinating that there are only three times in all of Scripture that the word *sweat* or *perspire* is mentioned. The first is in the Garden of Eden when Adam—and the entire human family—received the curse. The last is in the Garden of Gethsemane, when Jesus was about to receive that curse on Himself, on our behalf. He was in such anguish that "his sweat was like drops of blood falling to the ground." Jesus took the curse so that He could restore us to the blessing and purpose that God bestowed in the beginning. He sweat so that we would not need to.

Do you remember that famous resurrection scene when Peter and John ran to the tomb, and Peter went in first and discovered it was empty? John painstakingly notes in his gospel that the cloth that had been wrapped around the head of Jesus for His burial "was still lying in its place." That cloth was a handkerchief that was used to wipe perspiration off someone's brow. When people would die and be buried, their heads would be covered in a cloth. This act announced that their work was finished. No more sweat. When Jesus rose from the dead, He took the time to take that cloth off His head and put it back in its place. His work was finished. He did the work so we would not have to. He sweat blood for us.

The only other time sweat is mentioned in Scripture is in an obscure Old Testament passage in which God tells the priests that when they come into His presence, they are to wear linen, not wool, because "they shall not clothe themselves with anything that causes sweat."

One could get the idea that God does not like sweat. It is as if God says, "Don't show up and tell me that you earned salvation or any other good thing by the sweat of your brow. I sweat for you. Your job is to trust Me, lean into Me, yoke up with Me. I want you to have rest in your soul. I want you to learn the unforced rhythms of grace. I want you to live and work in My flow."

What does this mean for you? Most importantly, you must rest in the truth that you have been saved by grace through faith, not by works you have done or could do, but by the work that Jesus did. To believe in Jesus is to believe this, and to believe this is to have a deep-settled peace that permeates every aspect of your being. I know a lot of people who are gritted-teeth, fists-clenched, try-harder, anxious, sweaty-faced, not-quite believers because they do not fully trust that Jesus already did everything needed to be done to make them right with God. Trust Him.

Once that is resolved, you are then able to do the work God planned for you to do. You are not saved by your works, of course, but you are saved to do good works. You can only do those good works by grace. You can fulfill your purpose in a pre-curse, all-blessing, no-sweat reality as you learn to rest in Him even in your most challenging work.

So please . . . take a deep breath. As hard as you may be working to do good—to raise your kids, succeed at your job, finish school, run a nonprofit, or serve your church—God is working harder. Or rather, He already worked harder. He will not call you to do anything—anything!—that He will not give you the power to do. Wipe your brow, put the sweat cloth back in its place and get to work fulfilling your purpose in the energy of God's blessing.

Do you trust God to bless you as you do His work?

SECTION 2 NOTES

◼ CHAPTER 8: BLESSING AND PURPOSE

"Be fruitful and multiply": Genesis 1:27–28 NLT

"God saved you by his grace": Ephesians 2:8–10 NLT

"What I was made to do": *Man on Wire*, directed by James Marsh (BBC, Discovery Channel, UK Film Council, Wall to Wall Media and Red Box Films, 2008).

"The fixing of destinies": Walton, *The NIV Application Commentary: Genesis*, 597.

"Being transformed into his image": 2 Corinthians 3:18

"Missing the mark": Vine, Unger, and White, *Vine's Complete Expository Dictionary*, 576.

◼ CHAPTER 9: INVITATION TO ADVENTURE

"An adventure that I am arranging": J. R. R.Tolkien, *The Hobbit* (New York: Houghton Mifflin Harcourt, 2007), 6.

"Something Tookish woke up inside him": Tolkien, *The Hobbit*, 16.

"Work it and take care of it": Genesis 2:15

"Go from your country": Genesis 12:1–4

"This is almost like a second creation account": Longman, *How to Read Genesis* (Downers Grove, IL, InterVarsity Press, 2005), 127.

◼ CHAPTER 10: INDISPENSABLE YOU

"Before I formed you in the womb": Jeremiah 1:4–5

I was deeply moved when George W. Bush wrote: George W. Bush, *Decision Points* (New York: Random House, 2010), 60.

"Are not five sparrows": Luke 12:6–7

"I beg you to live in a way that is worthy": Ephesians 4:1 CEV

It is called Area of Destiny: An Area of Destiny assessment is available to you at www.terryasmith.com/AOD. You can explore your AOD in the domain of relationships, vocation and ministry, and merge what you learn to get a sense of the indispensable role you were made to play. Learn more about AOD in *The Hospitable Leader: Create Environments Where People and Dreams Flourish* (Minneapolis: Bethany House, 2018).

"Destined for our glory": 1 Corinthians 2:7

"The Spirit searches all things": 1 Corinthians 2:10

■ CHAPTER 11: SOMEDAY MORNING

"The holy and sure blessings promised to David": Acts 13:34

"Who am I . . . that you have brought me": 1 Chronicles 17:16–27 NLT

"I have found David": Acts 13:22

"David . . . is the kind of person who pleases me most!": Acts 13:22 CEV

"Went after it, struck it and rescued the sheep": 1 Samuel 17:35

"David ran quickly toward the battle line": 1 Samuel 17:48

"Be strong, act like a man": 1 Kings 2:2

"In worship on his bed": 1 Kings 1:47

"Have mercy on me, O God": Psalm 51:1–10

"Rich . . . unending blessings": Psalm 21:3–6

"You know what your servant is really like": 2 Samuel 7:20 NLT

■ CHAPTER 12: RISK AND REWARD

"God can bless you with everything": 2 Corinthians 9:6–8 CEV

"God is able to bless you abundantly": 2 Corinthians 9:8

"Since you have shown that you can be trusted": Luke 19:17 CEV

"Why didn't you put my money in the bank": Luke 19:23–26 CEV

"That's what I mean: Risk your life": Luke 19:26 MSG

"I assure you that everyone who has given up house": Mark 10:29–30 NLT

■ CHAPTER 13: RESISTANCE TRAINING

"Most of us have two lives": Steven Pressfield, *The War of Art: Break Through the Blocks and Win Your Inner Creative Battles* (New York: Rugged Land, 2002), front matter.

"Dear brothers and sisters": James 1:2–4 NLT

The opposite of happiness is not sadness: Timothy Ferriss, *The 4-Hour Workweek* (New York: Crown Publishing, 2007), 51.

"Will run from you": James 4:7 CEV

"Communication between a person and God": Terry A. Smith, *The Hospitable Leader* (Minneapolis: Bethany House Publishers, 2018), 149.

"In all these things we are more than conquerors": Romans 8:31–37

■ CHAPTER 14: NO SWEAT

"This is my work and I can do it": Colossians 1:29 TLB

"Take my yoke upon you": Matthew 11:29–30

"Walk with me and work with me": Matthew 11:28–30 MSG

"By the sweat of your brow you will eat": Genesis 3:19

"His sweat was like drops of blood": Luke 22:44

"They shall not clothe themselves": Ezekiel 44:18 NKJV

PEOPLE

fifteen

A Sacrament of Blessing

want to encourage you with this: the more you practice an intentional consciousness of how much God not only wants to bless you but also wants to bless other people through you, the more you will experience vast depths and fresh waves of overflowing blessing.

Jesus made it clear that my relationship with God is not just about my relationship with God. It is about my relationship with God *and* you. He is *our* Father. Jesus told us that the two most important things we can do is to love God and love others. He also told us that our love for one another is a true test of our love for Him. "As I have loved you, so you must love one another. By this will everyone know that you are my disciples."

In the spirit of this book, we might restate His words to read, "As I have blessed you, so you must bless one another." I believe this captures the heart of God. He wants to do good to you, in you and through you to others. If your blessing focus is on yourself, you will not be truly blessed. That is not how this blessing thing works.

Throughout Scripture, blessing came not only directly from God to people, but from people to people. We have the privilege of being able to mediate blessing from God to others. He literally blesses people through us.

The French and Christian philosopher Simone Weil wrote that the secret to connecting to God and understanding the meaning of life is to "pay attention." Her vision for this was informed by the command Jesus gave to "Love the Lord your God with all your heart and. . . . Love your neighbor as yourself." In response to the question, "Who is my neighbor?" Jesus told the story of the good Samaritan who came to a man wounded and lying on the side of the road. "And when he saw him, he took pity on him." The Samaritan did not just see this man in need, but he paid attention to him, he really saw him and he did what needed to be done to meet his need. By so doing, he loved both God and his neighbor.

Weil further asserts that this kind of seeing, this level of paying attention, is sacramental. I really like this: Paying attention, truly seeing another human being as a person to be loved as we are loved, blessed as we are blessed, is sacramental. A sacrament is a physical thing through which God conveys His presence, and He uses it for His purposes. The sacrament—or ordinance, if you prefer—of communion is an example of this. When we eat the bread and drink the wine remembering Jesus, focusing our attention on Jesus and believing in Jesus, then God's presence permeates that physical act, and we experience His life.

Your relationships can become a sacrament of blessing when you truly see the other person's need and potential and invoke God's blessing in their lives. God is present in a relationship like that. God's desire to do good is released in and through you in a relationship like that.

I pray that we can each pay full attention to how much the people around us need and want to be blessed by and through us. We must consciously concentrate on the people in our lives and purposely conduct God's presence and blessing through our flesh-and-blood relationships.

Yes, people can and are blessed directly by God, but God often uses physical things—in this case, human beings in relationship—as a conduit for blessing. Our children need to be blessed by us. Our spouse needs to be blessed by us. Our friends need to be blessed by us. Our teammates need to be blessed by us. Our neighbors need to be blessed by us.

If I bless another person, it means that I invoke and help bring God's blessing into their lives. I offer them unconditional love and acceptance. I let them know how valuable they are to God and to me. I speak good into their future in a way that has prophetic implications and shapes reality, and I act in ways to help bring that preferred future to pass. Dallas Willard said, "Blessing is ... the actual putting forth of your will for the good of another person."

I stand every Sunday morning, extend my hands toward my congregation and say the priestly "The Lord Bless You" benediction. But I do not think that is the only way, or even the primary way, to give someone else a blessing. Praying or speaking a blessing is incredibly important, but it is just as important to live our lives every day in a way that radiates blessing. When we really see people, when we project good intentions toward them, when we do good to them, when we help them grow closer to God and when we help them move toward their God-dreamed future, then the Lord has blessed them. You are an instrument of blessing.

Think of yourself as a blessing contagion who is infecting everyone around you with something supernatural and inexplicably wonderful. Daniel Goleman, author of groundbreaking books on emotional and social intelligence writes, "Emotions are contagious. . . . We transmit and catch moods from each other in what amounts to a subterranean economy of the psyche. . . . We catch feelings from one another as though they were some kind of social virus."

Our relationships affect much more than how we feel, however. They shape most everything about our lives.

Multiple studies have shown that if we are in relationship with people who are happy, we are much more likely to be happy. If we hang out with people who are physically and nutritionally healthy, we are much more likely to eat right, exercise and be healthy, too.

If we spend time with people who are learners, we are more likely to be learners. If we surround ourselves with people who are engaged in positive life transformation, we are more likely to be successful at positive life transformation. Which is to say, if you are blessed, the people around you will inevitably be blessed, too. You are infectious, a positive pandemic of blessing, and the people in your life cannot avoid catching the blessing that will be emanating from you.

The seminal blessing God gave Abraham was so powerful that it was passed from him to his children, to his grandchildren and ultimately through Jesus to us. The force of this blessing was not diminished by the passage of time nor by jumping from one bloodline to another.

I am thinking about how Abraham's grandson Jacob was so blessed that blessing overflowed into the house of his father-in-law and employer, Laban. Jacob was planning to leave Laban's employment, but Laban pleaded with him. "If I have found favor in your eyes please stay. . . . The Lord has blessed me because of you." He then added, "Name your wages, and I will pay them."

I am thinking about how Jacob's son Joseph was going through a really tough time as he was enslaved in the household of Potiphar in Egypt. Yet Potiphar "put him in charge of his household and of all that he owned, the LORD blessed the household of the Egyptian because of Joseph. The blessing of the LORD was on everything Potiphar had."

I am thinking about how eventually all of Egypt was blessed by Joseph's presence and how when Joseph brought his father, Jacob, into the presence of Pharaoh, "Jacob blessed Pharaoh." The blessing was so powerful in Abraham's family that everyone they associated with experienced the blessing flowing from them.

And I am thinking about you. Whether they know it or not, the people in your life are so fortunate. You are a living, breathing blessing transmitter. If you will pay attention to the people around you and be a willing vessel of blessing, blessing will pour from you to others. Your friends, your spouse, your children, your teammates, your employer, your employees and your neighbors will all be blessed because of you. You are a sacrament of blessing.

Will you increase your awareness today of how much God wants to use you to mediate His blessing to others?

sixteen

How to Give a Blessing

There is a blessing-sized void in every person's life that can only be filled by God and by the blessing that comes through His people. People like you and me.

I am deeply moved by the story of Isaac and the blessing he gave to his son Jacob rather than his son Esau. Isaac's words of blessing to Jacob are so beautiful.

> "Come here, my son, and kiss me. . . . Ah, the smell of my son is like the smell of a field that the LORD has blessed. May God give you heaven's dew and earth's richness—an abundance of grain and new wine. . . . May God Almighty bless you and make you fruitful and increase

your numbers. . . . May he give you and your descendants the blessing given to Abraham."

When Esau did not receive this blessing from his father, "he burst out with a loud and bitter cry and said to his father, 'Bless me—me too, my father.'" He did this even though he was grown and married and a certifiable tough guy. Later in Scripture we are told "he sought the blessing with tears."

Esau's desperation is a natural human response to disappointment at not receiving the blessing he needed and wanted.

Each of us has an instinctual desire to be blessed, first by God the Father, and then by our parents. To a lesser but still important degree, we desire blessing from those who have authority in our lives: our spouses, intimate friends and others with whom we are in meaningful relationships. I pray that you have your need for blessing satiated by those significant people in your life who have the power to bless you, and I challenge you to be an instrument of blessing to those in your life who need and want to be blessed by you.

On one hand, everyone with whom you come in contact should be blessed by God through you. Then there are those people in your life for whom you are a singularly important person, essential to satisfying their need for blessing. These are individuals who are desperate for the blessing that you carry, and you have the wonderful privilege and solemn obligation to make certain their blessing-sized void is filled.

The giving of a blessing in some cases might be a unique, one-time act, as was the case of Isaac and Jacob. For most of us, though, it should be a way of life. We can constantly bless those around us in a manner that ensures they never feel "unblessed." There have been a few signature moments in my life when my parents have spoken words of blessing over me, sometimes with the laying on of hands. But there really has never been a time when they were not extending blessing to me. My dad once inscribed a book he gave me with the words "to my son in whom I am well pleased." Many years later, I can still see in my mind his handwriting in blue ink penned on that page.

That is typical of the ways large and small that my folks have and continue to bless me. "We love you. We are so proud of you. You are a good man. You are a good son and a good father. God has great things in store for you. We are praying for you." Even in my sixth decade, their blessing still matters, and I am grateful to receive it.

If you are in need of the blessing of a father or mother or some other significant person in your life but it has not yet been given, ask them for it. If they are unable to offer it, seek it elsewhere. I once flew all the way to South America in part because I wanted a particular pastor there to lay his hands on me, to pray for me and to bless me.

While he prayed for me, I felt called to go on a 21-day fast, which was not exactly what I was looking for in that moment. But those 21 days became a means of grace that have informed my life and ministry for more than 25 years. Seek the blessing you need and want.

If you are in a relationship where you are the one who needs to bestow a blessing, offer it urgently and generously. Interestingly, Isaac lived for many years—perhaps as many as forty years—after he gave his blessing to Jacob. Yet he was aware he was getting older and sensed an urgency to give his blessing. He, therefore, took insistent action and gave it. When he knew what he needed to do, he did not wait. And then he got to live long enough to see his blessing begin to be manifested in both Jacob's life and the life of his family.

You may have someone in your life to whom you need to give your blessing in a formal way. Perhaps you might take advantage of some rite of passage or a life celebration such as a wedding or signature birthday. Maybe you can create some unique occasion to offer your blessing. Follow the biblical pattern of laying your hands on that person or touching them in some other appropriate and meaningful way.

When Jacob blessed his grandsons, he put them on his knees, he kissed and embraced them and then he laid his hands on their heads. When people brought children to Jesus, "he took the children in his arms, placed his hands on them and blessed them."

Speak words that convey unconditional love and that express how much that person is valued. Be specific about some praiseworthy things that he or she has done and detail a positive quality you have observed. Speak in faith about good things you see for his or her future, and then articulate ways you intend to act to help that future come to pass. Most importantly, invoke God's presence. Ultimately it is His blessing that people most desperately need.

You probably have many people in your life who need your blessing in a less formal way. Find ways to bless with intentionality. When God blessed Abraham, he told him, "All peoples on earth will be blessed through you." We need to bring blessing to "all peoples" in all kinds of ways.

It is also important to note that we not only have the power to bless, but we also have the power to curse. To curse might mean to speak and act in a manner that unleashes negative or dark potentialities. To curse could also mean to simply leave people without a blessing, left on their own in this fallen world. Is it possible that not blessing someone when it is within our power to do so is effectively cursing them?

Proverbs tells us that our words can bring life or death. I also think our lack of words—in this case, a lack of blessing—could bring death, or at least something less than the life in all of its fullness God intended. Choose not to leave someone with a blessing-shaped hole in his or her life when God ordained you to fill it.

Who is someone you believe you need to bless in some significant way?

seventeen

The Kiss Still Works

Y

A surgeon shared his heart-rending experience of removing a tumor from a young woman's cheek, and how, though he tried "with religious fervor" to limit the damage to her face, a twig of the nerve to the muscles of her mouth was severed. After the surgery he stood at her bedside and was crestfallen to see "her face postoperative, her mouth twisted in palsy, clownish." Her husband stood on the opposite side of the bed and gazed at his wife and her distorted mouth with unquestioned love.

The young wife asked the doctor, "Will my mouth always be like this?" He replied that it would, that the nerve was cut. She lay there in silence. The young man smiled.

"I like it," he said. "It is kind of cute."

The surgeon wrote elegantly, "At once, I know who he is. I understand and lower my gaze. One is not bold in an encounter with a god." Then the young man bowed low to kiss his wife's crooked mouth, and the doctor was close enough to see "how he twists his own lips to accommodate hers, to show her that their kiss still works."

When I read this story, I cannot help but think of the incarnation. Through Jesus, the God of the universe bowed low to assume the nature and form of a human being. He did this so that He could meet us in our damaged and wounded condition and demonstrate His love for us.

When God created human beings in His own image, He wanted to look at men and women and see His own reflection. He wanted to smile and see us mirror His smile back. Because of sin, though, the God image was distorted, and the human smile became crooked, at best. But God, who was determined to bless the people He had made, rearranged Himself into a form that could kiss our twisted smile. "The Word became human and lived among us." He continued to be who He had always been and yet "made himself nothing" and was "made in human likeness" so that He could show us His love.

Jesus is the embodiment of all of God's desire to bless us. God has "blessed us in the heavenly realms with every spiritual blessing in Christ." In the beginning, when God blessed Adam and Eve, He surely articulated some version of how blessings were spoken throughout Scripture. I imagine He told them He loved them, valued them, had a purpose for them, planned a wonderful future for them and would work to help bring that future to pass, if they would let Him. They rejected His blessing, of course, and chose the curse instead. This injured the entire human family.

In the incarnation, God was saying that He had found a way to meet us in our scarred condition. He devised a way to match His holiness to our marred humanity. In Jesus, "mercy and truth have met together; righteousness and peace have kissed." Through Jesus, God manifested Himself to bring the blessing He always intended.

Through Jesus, He declared, "I still love you, still value you, still have a purpose for you and still have a wonderful future for you. If you will just believe in Me and be in relationship with Me—kiss Me back!—I will work in and through you to bring that future to pass."

I suggest that just as God humbled Himself to meet us in our disfigured reality, we must do whatever it takes to meet people wherever they are, in whatever condition they are in, so that we can curse the curse and bring them blessing. Sometimes we must bow low and twist our mouth to match God's blessing to others. "In your relationships with one another, have the same mindset as Christ Jesus: Who, being in very nature God . . . made himself nothing by taking the very nature of a servant, being made in human likeness." What would it look like for us to have the mindset of Jesus in our insistence to bring blessing to others, especially those people in our lives who desperately need blessing but have done little, or nothing, to deserve it?

None of us have done anything to deserve God's blessing, yet He contorted Himself into a human body. He did for us what we could not do and gave us what we did not earn. This should shape our attitude about the people in our lives who have not lived up to our expectations or have rejected our attempts to help them. We should think about that when we face people over whom it might be difficult to speak words of affirmation because they are not doing much that we can affirm. They have crooked smiles, not because of someone else's decisions or mistakes, but because of their own. Can you find a way to get in a position to bless those types of people? Can you kiss their crooked mouths?

This Scripture in Hebrews intrigues me: "By faith Isaac blessed Jacob and Esau in regard to their future." We learned in the last chapter that Esau did not receive the blessing that established the bloodline through which Abraham's blessing would flow. But he did receive a blessing from his father. Part of that blessing was that Esau would not forever be ruled by Jacob, but I assume there was more than that.

Isaac loved Esau deeply and must have shown him affection and spoken words of affirmation to him. He must have supported him in practical ways as he moved toward his future. He blessed Esau despite the fact that Esau was less than perfect. He lacked impulse control, for instance—remember the bowl of porridge?—and he brought grief to his parents by his choice of wife. But this is typical of the human condition. His deceitful brother, Jacob, certainly had his issues, as well.

Yet Isaac found a way to bless both of his sons "in regard to their future," and not necessarily because of what he saw in them or knew about them. He blessed them because of what he wanted for them and what he believed for them. He blessed them by faith, and he figured out a way to bless them both.

You might have a teenager who is in a season that feels plagued or an adult child whose decisions have brought you grief; or perhaps on another level you see little in your spouse to affirm right now or have a friend you feel estranged from because of some choices they have made; or you are in some other significant relationship with someone who seems "unblessable." But Jesus brought us God's blessing even in our utter depravity. "God demonstrates his own love for us in this; while we were still sinners, Christ died for us." How might that have an impact on the way you think about loving others who need your blessing, particularly those who may seem unlovable?

We need to realize our potential to change the apparently unblessable person into a blessed person, because of actions we take to bless them in faith. In Fyodor

Dostoevsky's classic *The Brothers Karamazov*, Ivan, a cynical and unbelieving intellectual, tries to convince his younger brother and passionate Christ follower, Alyosha, that Jesus is the source of the world's problems and that He is not worthy of being followed. Ivan tells a story in which he imagines Jesus imprisoned during the Inquisition in sixteenth-century Spain by the evil Grand Inquisitor who hurls terrible accusations at Him. When he finishes his harangue, the Grand Inquisitor waits, expecting Jesus to reply in kind. Instead, Jesus walks over to the embittered old man and kisses his sallow lips. All He offers in response to His accuser is a kiss. Ivan portrayed this as weakness.

When he finished with his story, Ivan stood hoping for a response from Alyosha that would indicate that Ivan had been successful in his attempt to undermine his brother's faith. But "Alyosha stood up, went over to him in silence, and gently kissed him on the lips." Alyosha, understanding the power of divine, self-sacrificing love, imitated Jesus, the divine lover. And Ivan was utterly disarmed by his kiss.

Dostoevsky's story is fiction, and yet it is based in truth. God's response to the evil that damaged His world was a kiss of love. He knew that doing whatever was necessary to match His love to hurting people was the answer the world really needs. It is as if God said, "Regardless what you say or do, I am going to bow low to kiss you." His kiss is redeeming the world and bringing us His blessing.

You may have someone in your life who has disappointed you, provoked you or injured you. You may know someone who needs your blessing, but they have made it difficult for you to give it. Perhaps your blessing is the very thing God will use to bring them transformation and give you peace. Meet them and bless them in their present condition. As the apostle Peter encouraged, "Greet one another with a kiss of love."

Who is someone you need to "bow low" and "twist your lips" to bless today?

eighteen

The First Institution
of Blessing

When the Creator addressed the first human beings, He "blessed *them*." He had decided it was not good for a person to be alone, so He united the first man and woman as husband and wife "and they became one flesh. Adam and his wife were both naked, and they felt no shame."

This is not to say that God does not bless individuals, of course. He clearly loves each of us as His children, and He blesses each of us, married or single. It is to say that His first blessing was for people who were in relationship with one another, specifically this man and wife. It seems important to focus for a minute on marriage and family, and hopefully we can also apply these truths to other covenant relationships in our lives.

The family is the first institution God ordained. Its purposes are many, but one is that the family was the first place of blessing. It is elemental to blessing today. In the Genesis story, God blessed Adam and Eve together, "then God blessed Noah and his sons," then God blessed Abraham, and through him, God blessed generations of his children, who ultimately brought us Jesus. All of us are in families, and a big part of God's plan is that blessing should happen in families and through families. We might say the family is the first institution of blessing.

One cannot help but love the family celebrated in Proverbs 31 that features a wife and mother of "noble character." "Her husband has full confidence in her and lacks nothing of value. She brings him good, not harm, all the days of her life. . . . Her children arise and call her blessed; her husband also, and he praises her."

I see an explosion of blessing in this home, blessing ricocheting everywhere, even as this woman watches over the affairs of her household, builds successful businesses, serves the poor and more. It is abundantly clear that the foundation of this blessed family is a marriage of interdependent blessing: the husband doing good to his wife, the wife doing good to her husband.

Families come in all shapes and sizes. I have seen many single moms and dads create environments of extreme blessing in their homes. I have watched aunts, uncles, grandparents and surrogate parents bless children in ways akin to the Genesis patriarchs. I have witnessed numerous spiritual fathers and mothers impart innumerable blessings to spiritual children of all ages. Let's focus on the scriptural ideal, however, that the foundation of the family is the relationship between husband and wife, mother and father. This partnership was the focus of blessing in the beginning, and blessed marriages continue to be fundamentally important to God's plan to bless the world.

There are few things as wonderful or mysterious as love and mutual blessing between husband and wife. We learn in Ephesians that the mystery of self-sacrificial love in a marriage is so wonderful that through it we can learn about Christ. We can observe a love so great that He was motivated to give His life for the Church. This is an outrageous love, and this love is integral to the kind of marriage God can bless. It is integral to a marriage in which a husband and a wife do good to one another and their children over a lifetime.

Love can no more be fully comprehended or explained than God, "because God is love." Yet we should attempt to learn all we can about God and love, particularly the love that fuels a successful marriage. Cornell professor Robert Sternberg proposes that "consummate love" can be viewed as an equilateral triangle, equal amounts of three components: commitment, intimacy and passion. I like this theory of love.

Commitment is the most important part of marital love. Marriage is a covenant, the promise a man and woman make to give their lives to one another till death do them part. They vow to do good to each other, regardless of feeling or circumstance. In the first book of Corinthians, we learn that love is patient, kind, does not envy, boast or dishonor, is not proud, self-seeking or easily angered, keeps no record of wrongs, always protects, trusts, hopes and perseveres. C. S. Lewis wrote that love is an act of the will:

> Love . . . is not merely a feeling. It is a deep unity, maintained by the will and deliberately strengthened by habit. . . . They can have this love for each other even at those moments when they do not like each other. . . . It is on this love that the engine of marriage is run.

This undying commitment is essential to genuine love. Thankfully, however, there is much more to a blessed marriage than just the promises we make. *Intimacy* is about knowing another person in the depths of their soul. When we are told the first husband and wife were naked and unashamed, the Bible is giving us more than a reference to physical nakedness. Shame is rooted in the soul. They had naked souls; they truly knew one another.

Part of love is knowing and being known, and in marriage, this is an endless adventure. As I write this, I have been married to the love of my life for 39 years. One of my greatest joys and greatest challenges is that I know her so well, yet there is so much more of her to know. Marriage is a lifetime exploration of another human being. This process must be intentional and caring. As Paul wrote, "This is my prayer: that your love may abound more and more in knowledge and depth of insight."

And then there is *passion*—and thank God for it. When I meditate on how a marriage should reflect the love of Jesus for the Church, I envision a shocking, emotive, all-consuming love. I am concerned that sometimes in our Christian emphasis on the commitment of covenant, we downplay romance, mystery and excitement. The wise father in Proverbs counseled his son to "rejoice in the wife of your youth. . . . May her breasts satisfy you always, may you ever be intoxicated with her love." Intoxicated! We should be satisfied with nothing less than inebriating love. We must do whatever work is necessary to keep the flame—the passion—of first love ever-burning brightly.

The story of Elizabeth Barrett and Robert Browning captures something of the beauty of commitment, intimacy and passion dancing in concert to create consummate love and mutual blessing. Elizabeth wrote a collection of poems in 1844 that were read by Robert, a poet himself, that so moved him that he wrote her a letter.

Having never met or seen her, he declared, "I do, as I say, love these books with all my heart—and I love you too."

He fell in love with her through the words that flowed from her soul. Robert was a robust 36-year-old man. He did not know that Elizabeth, at age 40, was a virtual invalid who, because of chronic illness, had not left the upstairs of her father's house for more than a year. Yet after they met, then courted through writing some six hundred letters back and forth, they ran away and got married.

And Elizabeth was healed slowly through the elixir of Robert's wholehearted love. She then wrote him another poem, immortal words attempting to express the depths of incomprehensible love.

> How do I love thee? Let me count the ways. I love thee to the depth and breadth and height my soul can reach. . . . I love thee with a love I seemed to lose . . . with the breath, smiles, tears, of all my life!—and if God choose, I shall but love thee better after death.

Never underestimate the inestimable power of love.

The love between a man and wife is blessed by God, and it is the foundation of a home where there is blessing all around. Perhaps you are in a season of challenge in your marriage. If so, I encourage you to work on your relationship in faith that God will supernaturally bless it. Perhaps you are in a season of harmony in your marriage.

Expect explosions of blessing. Perhaps you are not married. If that is the case, you can apply the truths in this chapter to your relationships and know that God will find all kinds of ways to bless you and bless other people through you.

Regardless of your state or season, what actions can you take to grow in love and build relationships of mutual blessing?

nineteen

Strong Environments
of Blessing

P astor and theologian Dietrich Bonhoeffer founded
the Finkenwalde Seminary in 1935 to train Christian leaders to preach the Gospel and oppose Adolf
Hitler and the Nazis. Some of his contemporaries were
critical of the unwavering discipleship and rigorous spiritual discipline that he required of the seminarians. These
disciplines, however, were inspiring the students to have a
joyful and robust faith in Jesus and an enthusiastic practice of His teachings. One detractor came for a visit, and
Bonhoeffer took him to a place where they could see a
Nazi training ground in the distance. Fighter planes were
thunderously taking off and landing, and soldiers were

being trained en masse for warfare. An impassioned Bonhoeffer explained that he was trying to build a spiritual army at Finkenwalde that would be mightier than the evil powers of Nazism. "You have to be stronger than these tormentors you find everywhere today."

Most of us are painfully aware that we live in a world that is still reeling from the curse and is infected with evil seemingly everywhere. Scripture tells us we must "overcome evil with good." The antidote to the strength of the curse is a stronger dose of blessing. I hear constantly from parents and others who share the same concern for children. We share a desire to inoculate children from the curse-induced negative forces that seem so pervasive.

How, we ask, can our kids survive and succeed in this dark world? This wilderness? I propose that people of faith who hold Christian values create such strong environments of blessing that blessing overwhelms the injurious capacity of evil. Have no doubt—the blessing of God is infinitely more potent than the worst sickness of the curse. When we bring blessing, we find that victory over every adversarial potentiality is inevitable.

My parents engendered such an attractive atmosphere in our home that I felt little allure to live out of alignment with the faith and values they raised me with. I felt sorry for my peers who did not follow Jesus, who did not attend church and who did not strive to live according to the Judeo-Christian values rooted in Scripture.

Proverbs tells us, "Train up a child in the way he should go, and when he is old he will not depart from it." Raymond Ortlund's comments on this famous proverb are enlightening. "The Hebrew word translated 'train up' is related to an Arabic verb that was used of rubbing the palate of a newborn child with a date mixture, to get the child to suck." The idea was to give a child something sweet to taste so they would want more. A home full of blessing is a magnetic force that is constantly drawing everyone in it to more blessing and more of God, from whom all blessings flow. This greatly enhances the possibility that children will move toward the life God dreams for them. "Taste and see that the LORD is good; blessed is the one who takes refuge in him."

We must learn to pass blessing from generation to generation. This process is more than speaking a patriarchal or matriarchal blessing over our children, important as that is. It is telling our children God's story and teaching biblical values in an attractive environment. It is training children in the way they should go in a climate of blessing. I write this to parents and anyone who cares about passing blessing into the future.

Author Mark Gerson makes a compelling case that religious education of children in the home as commanded by Moses is the primary reason the Jews have made such a positive and disproportionate contribution to humanity over many millennia. The blessing of Abraham has been passed from generation to generation, not only through prophetic impartation, but also by parents doing the hard work of explaining God's story and teaching His commandments.

Gerson's book *The Telling* is about the *Haggadah*, the Jewish text that sets forth the order of the Passover Seder. It details how Jewish parents are to tell the story of the exodus. In the urgent and existential rush out of Egypt, Moses took valuable time to stress that what God had done must be repeatedly recounted to future generations. "And when your children ask you, 'What does this ceremony mean to you?' then tell them, 'It is the Passover sacrifice to the LORD, who passed over the houses of the Israelites in Egypt and spared our homes.'"

Later Moses made it clear they were not just to tell God stories, but they were also to teach His commands. "These commandments that I give you today are to be on your hearts. Impress them on your children. Talk about them when you sit at home and when you walk along the road, when you lie down and when you get up."

I submit that parents must accept primary responsibility to educate their children in the faith and primary responsibility for their children's moral instruction. Gerson writes:

Jewish communities had a robust educational system thousands of years before anyone else in the world believed in having one. Still, education was never a function that could be outsourced. The questions in the Haggadah are asked by children, but they are not answered by teachers, rabbis, or anyone else. They are answered by parents.

One of the most important roles of a parent is that of being a teacher. The book of Proverbs, for instance, is premised on a mom and dad teaching their child that to live successfully is to understand the wisdom of God. "Listen, my son, to your father's instruction and do not forsake your mother's teaching." "Bind them always on your heart; fasten them around your neck." Do you want to pass God's blessings to your children? You must do more than pray; you must also teach.

My wife and I made the kitchen table a focal point of education for our children as my wife and I raised them. We were a family that was eating, laughing, telling stories, sometimes arguing and just doing life together. But we always used every opportunity to make Jesus and His teachings the center of everything, many times without our children realizing this was deliberate. Please do not let secular educational institutions, the media or social media, celebrity culture or anyone or anything, regardless of how well-meaning they might be, supplant you in your God-given role as the teacher in your home.

Even the Church is limited in its capacity to do all that is necessary to lead your kids to a truly blessed life.

But you can do it. You must do it. You cannot determine outcomes for your kids, but you can cultivate a sweet tooth for a good God, His better story and the good He will do in their lives if they live His way.

Let me leave this discussion that has been centered on the home with three words—fun, discipline and destiny.

Fun. It is not accidental that the story of God and Passover is recounted at a feast. A Seder dinner is both sacred and fun. Family, food, wine, conversation, stories and games. Blessing is transmitted in this kind of atmosphere. We must create a stronger and more attractive environment than any other alternative in the world around us in order to impart God's truth.

Discipline. Scripture teaches that if we love our children, we will discipline them. Our kids need to lovingly be taught right and wrong and to be held accountable when they make wrong choices. They need parents to guide them in the right way to live—God's way to live. Do not buy into a misguided culture that celebrates children parenting parents. Your kids need you to show them the way to a blessed life. Ultimately, of course, discipline will bring them freedom.

Destiny. One of the keys to *this* being more attractive than *that* is to live with an awareness that we were created, blessed and purposed by a good God who has a wonderful plan for our lives. Training up a child in the way they should go is not just about moral direction. It is also about destiny. Our children need to know that if they move in the direction that God planned for them, they will live life in all of its fullness—a truly blessed life.

Are you willing to accept the responsibility of training future generations to live in God's full blessing?

Bless Who?

Here is a hard saying of Jesus, at least for me: "Love your enemies, do good to those who hate you, bless those who curse you, pray for those who mistreat you." He also says that anyone can love someone who loves them and do good to those who do good to them, but those of us who follow Him must go further than that. We who are blessed are obligated to bless even our enemies.

You would think that a person who was blessed would be enemy-free. Sometimes, however, it feels as if the more blessed you are, the more enemies you have. Jesus had an amazing array of people who opposed Him, and He appears to assume that you will have enemies, too. Do not be surprised by this. There are dark spiritual forces and fallen-world realities that incite some people to respond to all the good in you and the good happening through you in antagonistic ways. There is a spiritual root to this, but regardless of how you get at it, this is just the way the world is. You will have enemies.

An enemy could be as relatively innocuous as a neighbor who finds every opportunity to draw you into some ridiculous conflict. It could be as significant as a person of influence who actively opposes you and your dream with vindictive hostility. I have had nagging enemies, devastating enemies and all kinds of enemies in between. I continue to be challenged by the command of Jesus when He tells us to bless and not curse. More than that, though, I am grateful for His words, because I have learned that a blessing can turn an enemy into a friend.

I know a wonderful couple who was in a season of marriage so difficult that they came to see the other as an enemy. The wife told me she was so angry that her prayers became curses against her husband. Then she sensed Jesus, through the Holy Spirit, gently remind her to bless her husband, especially during all the acrimony. She was not to curse him.

She responded, "I don't want him to be blessed. I want him to get right."

The still, small voice replied, *"If you bless him, I will make things right. Part of how I will do good to him is to correct him. Pray for him and not against him. Bless him.*

I will make things right." And she did begin to bless her husband, and God did lead him to make things right.

When you become an agent of blessing to your enemies, God will do good to them, in them and through them, and it is quite possible the time will come when they will also bless you, pray for you and do good to you. This being true, we should desperately hope that our enemies will be truly blessed.

Then there are enemies who, because they have free will, continue to curse you regardless of your attempts to bless them. They have willfully chosen to reject God's entreaties and your efforts to do them good. Place this in God's hands.

> Do not repay anyone evil for evil. . . . As far as it depends on you, live at peace with everyone. Do not take revenge, my dear friends, but leave room for God's wrath. . . . "If your enemy is hungry, feed him; if he is thirsty, give him something to drink. In doing this, you will heap burning coals on his head." Do not be overcome by evil, but overcome evil with good.

You can only control your actions, and your job is to bless and not curse. Leave the rest to God.

One of my favorite words is *magnanimous*. To be magnanimous is to be generous to someone despite the injury they have inflicted on you. When I think of magnanimity,

I think of well-known larger-than-life figures such as Abraham Lincoln, Nelson Mandela and Martin Luther King Jr.

Abraham Lincoln populated his cabinet with political rivals to help bring the unity needed for the Union to win the Civil War. Nelson Mandela was elected president after an unjust 27-year imprisonment in apartheid South Africa. He then invited one of his white prison wardens to the inauguration and "overcame a personal mistrust bordering on loathing to share both power and a Nobel Peace Prize with the white president who preceded him." Martin Luther King Jr. insisted vehemently on a non-violent fight for civil rights in opposition to the violence perpetrated against him and his righteous cause.

Each of these men, however, pointed to Jesus as the ultimate example of magnanimity. Jesus turned the universe upside down. Even when He was insulted and abused in the most horrific ways, He refused to respond in kind. In the most eternally consequential and literal terms possible, Jesus defeated evil by doing good.

Reconciliation has to do with turning an enemy into a friend. This is what Jesus did on the cross when He blessed rather than cursed. "While we were God's enemies, we were reconciled to him through the death of his Son." We have now been given the "ministry of reconciliation." Through our actions, we can give people the opportunity to be reconciled both to God and to us. Reconciliation is for enemies. To reconcile, we must practice a Holy Spirit–led magnanimity that loves our enemies, does good to those who hate us, blesses those who curse us and prays for those who mistreat us. This is what Jesus did for us, and He empowers us to do it for others.

Some time ago, I experienced something life-altering around this idea. I had a relationship with someone over many years. This was someone I cared about deeply, but who had taken advantage of me in any number of ways over the years. They had hurt me in a manner I find hard to explain.

I made a decision to take a more disciplined and careful approach to the relationship for my good and, I believed, for this person's good as well. Though I still believe it is right to establish needed boundaries, in this situation, I took it too far. Over time, I became aware that my distance had hurt the other person and further damaged our relationship. We were not enemies in the classical sense, but there certainly was an unhealthy alienation.

One day I was praying the words of a song that I love that asks if God's patience will last even when I let Him down. I was asking God to show me grace, even though I continued to sin against Him. Then I saw this person in my mind saying the same words to me. "Will your patience run out if I let you down? I know that I have sinned against you and that my words have been tangled with lies. But you take brokenness and make it beautiful."

And I began to weep. I knew God's grace would not run out—would never run out—when I let God down, and I knew my response to the person who had repeatedly let me down needed to be the same.

In that moment, I was impressed to perform an outrageous act of generosity toward that person that I knew would bless them in a significant area of need in their life. And I did. And that relationship has moved from simmering hostility to something truly beautiful. Not perfect, but beautiful. Less wilderness, more Eden, if you have been tracking with me.

Is there some relationship in your life in which you need to change your posture from cursing to blessing? Can you possibly transform an enemy into a friend?

twenty-one

One New Humanity

The exquisitely written 133rd Psalm teaches a truth of paramount importance. "How good and pleasant it is when God's people live together in unity. . . . For there the LORD bestows his blessing." Along with these words that frame the song, the psalmist likens unity to precious anointing oil that was poured on the head of the high priest, Aaron, that ran down his beard and clothing, as well as to the falling dew of Mount Hermon that nurtures lush vegetation. He intimates that this is what it is like when God's people worship in unity. That is where God's blessing is pouring, running, falling and bringing life now and forever. God bestows His blessing on His people when we come together as one.

One of the themes of the writings of the apostle Paul in the New Testament is that Jesus not only came to make peace between people and God, but He also came to help people make peace with each other. In Ephesians, Paul deals explicitly with the abject hostility that existed in the first century between Jews and Gentiles. This volatile animus has played out over centuries, and we still see its effects in the world today, including cataclysmic events as recent as the Holocaust.

Jews and Gentiles were now members of Jesus and one another. Because of this, they were a model of what God wanted to accomplish through Jesus between all peoples in the world. Paul writes magnificently:

> Now in Christ Jesus you who once were far away have been brought near by the blood of Christ. For he himself is our peace, who has made the two groups one and has destroyed the barrier, the dividing wall of hostility. . . . His purpose was to create in himself one new humanity out of two, thus making peace, and in one body to reconcile both of them to God through the cross, by which he put to death their hostility.

One new humanity. This frequently comes to mind on Sundays, when I look out at the congregation that I serve in the suburbs of New York City. I see people from a wide variety of nations, races and ethnicities,

Republicans, Democrats and Independents, rich and not so rich, highly educated and not as educated, Pentecostals, Baptists, Presbyterians, Lutherans, Catholics and a variety of other denominations, along with many previously unchurched people. And yes, this also includes Jews alongside Gentiles.

And this one new humanity comes to mind when I witness Christ followers who appear to have become confused about their primary identity in Christ, people who misguidedly think of themselves first in terms of their national citizenship, race, political party, denominational background or gender rather than as "citizens of heaven." I myself am at times tempted to identify in some way other than as a Christian first, who is united with all believers regardless of our temporal, eternally unimportant differences. This mentality is a blessing blocker.

What is eternally important is what Jesus really came for. His number-one priority was to reconcile us to God and one another and to "create in himself one new humanity." Anything that hinders that project does damage to the thing God most wants to do. This is not to say that secondary identities such as race, ethnicity, doctrinal distinctives or political views do not matter. Paul, for instance, continued to identify as a Jew, yet he made it clear that his Jewishness was not as important as his oneness with all God's people everywhere, regardless of their secondary identities. He cautioned us to focus on the indisputable essentials of our faith and not to judge each other over "disputable matters" or to emphasize anything else that might divide us.

Paul's encouragement to the Ephesians, and to all of us, is that if God can tear down the wall of hostility between Jew and Gentile, He can reconcile any two people, or people groups, through the unifying power of the cross. He wrote about this even more expansively to the Colossians in response to those who were infecting the church in Colossae with sins of disunity. "Here there is no Gentile or Jew, circumcised or uncircumcised, barbarian, Scythian, slave or free, but Christ is all, and is in all." Again, Paul contrasts those who had plenty of human reasons not to care for one another at all, yet here they were sitting in the same church and hearing these words read together. Paul went on:

> Therefore, as God's chosen people, holy and dearly loved, clothe yourselves with compassion, kindness, humility, gentleness and patience. Bear with each other and forgive one another if any of you has a grievance against someone. Forgive as the Lord forgave you. And over all these virtues put on love, which binds them all together in perfect unity.

What glorious possibility is embedded in these words! I am both convicted and encouraged as I share them with you. I saw this lived out in an amazing way several years ago on one of the visits I made to Rwanda, Africa. The Rwandan genocide in 1994 when the majority Hutus massacred some 800,000 minority Tutsis in four months was one of the most horrific episodes of evil in history. The reconciliation that has taken place in Rwanda since the end of the genocide is one of the most hopeful stories in history.

I was invited to speak to pastors and leaders in a series of meetings in several churches in a Rwandan diocese that was hosted by a popular and charismatic Anglican bishop. He happened to be a Tutsi. One of the churches in which we spoke was in a little village so deep in the jungle that I was told that some of the villagers had never seen a white man before.

At the end of a long day of teaching, we had dinner in the pastor's two-room, block-wall, dirt-floor, tin-roof home. A feast was prepared on a charcoal fire in the yard, and warm milk was provided from the cow I could hear mooing just outside the glassless window. There were about thirty of us, mostly pastors, and we all washed our hands in one bucket that was passed around the room.

Please do not think less of me, but I must confess that I am somewhat of a germaphobe. As gracious and selfless as our hosts were, I struggled more than a little with the unfamiliar hygienic standards. When the food was placed on the table, it looked as if it was covered with raisins. I realized, however, that the raisins were moving. They were actually hordes of flies.

Even still, when I was invited to get my food, I took a generous portion and ate it as if it was the best meal I had ever enjoyed. They all watched, and it was truly wonderful, flies and all. I was pretty proud of my courageous hygienic-oblivious performance, which in retrospect is silly for so many reasons.

But it was truly heroic when I learned that the bishop was the only Tutsi in a house full of Hutus and had been cautioned to not travel to that village for fear of his safety, particularly for fear of the possibility of eating poisoned food. Yet regardless of that, and regardless of that fact that he had lost loved ones in the genocide, he feasted, laughed and encouraged his Hutu brothers and sisters in Christ as if he was at the marriage supper of the Lamb. Dividing walls of hostility? Torn down. Forgiveness? Built up. Love? Binding "all together in perfect unity."

Look, friend, if Hutu and Tutsi Christians in Rwanda can be reconciled, if Jew and Gentile believers in Ephesus can make peace, if all those different people in Colossae could do life together, then surely black, white and Latino, Chinese, Russian and American, Democrat, Republican and Independent, Baptist and Pentecostal, and all men and women who believe in Jesus can live together in unity and experience the blessing God bestows when we do. We are, after all, His "one new humanity." How good and pleasant it is.

How can you help create unity with other believers today?

SECTION 3 NOTES

CHAPTER 15: A SACRAMENT OF BLESSING

"As I have loved you, so you must love": John 13:34–35

The meaning of life is to "pay attention": Simone Weil, "Reflections on the Right Use of School Studies," TheMathesonTrust.org, https://www.themathesontrust.org/papers/christianity/Weil-Reflections.pdf.

"Love the Lord your God": Matthew 22:37

"And when he saw him, he took pity": Luke 10:33

"Blessing is . . . the actual putting forth": Dallas Willard, "The Right Way to Give Someone a Blessing," *Christianity Today*, January 8, 2014, https://www.christianitytoday.com/ct/2014/january-february/right-way-to-give-someone-blessing.html.

"Emotions are contagious": Daniel Goleman, *Social Intelligence* (New York: Random House, 2006), 114–115.

"If I have found favor in your eyes please stay": Genesis 30:27

"Name your wages": Genesis 30:28

"Put him in charge of his household": Genesis 39:5

"Jacob blessed Pharaoh": Genesis 47:10

CHAPTER 16: HOW TO GIVE A BLESSING

"Come here, my son, and kiss me": Genesis 27:26–28:4

"He burst out with a loud and bitter cry": Genesis 27:34

"He sought the blessing with tears": Hebrews 12:17

When Jacob blessed his grandsons: Genesis 48:9–14

"He took the children in his arms": Mark 10:16. My thinking in this section was influenced by John Trent and Gary Smalley, *The Blessing* (Nashville: Thomas Nelson, 2019).

"All peoples on earth will be blessed": Genesis 12:3

Our words can bring life or death: Proverbs 18:21

CHAPTER 17: THE KISS STILL WORKS

A surgeon shared his heart-rending experience: Richard Selzer, *Moral Lessons* (New York: Simon and Schuster, 1974), 45–46.

"The Word became human": John 1:14 NCV

"Made himself nothing": Philippians 2:7

"Blessed us in the heavenly realms": Ephesians 1:3

"Mercy and truth have met together": Psalm 85:10 NKJV

"In your relationships with one another": Philippians 2:5–7

"By faith Isaac blessed Jacob and Esau": Hebrews 11:20

We learned in the last chapter that Esau: Genesis 27:40

He blessed Esau despite the fact: Genesis 26:34–35

"God demonstrates His own love for us in this": Romans 5:8

"Alyosha stood up, went over to him": Fyodor Dostoevsky, *The Brothers Karamazov,* trans. Richard Pevear and Larissa Volokhonsky (New York: Farrar, Straus and Giroux, 1990).

"Greet one another with a kiss": 1 Peter 5:18

CHAPTER 18: THE FIRST INSTITUTION OF BLESSING

When the Creator addressed the first human beings, He "blessed *them*" (emphasis added): Genesis 1:28

"And they became one flesh": Genesis 2:24–25

"Then God blessed Noah and his sons": Genesis 9:1

A wife and mother of "noble character": Proverbs 31

"Her husband has full confidence in her": Proverbs 31:12–28

We learn in Ephesians that the mystery: Ephesians 5:21–33

"Because God is love": 1 John 4:8

"Consummate love" can be viewed as an equilateral triangle: Robert Sternberg, "Duplex Theory of Love: Triangular Theory of Love and Theory of Love as a Story," RobertJSternberg.com, 2018, http://www .robertjsternberg.com/love.

Love is patient, kind: 1 Corinthians 13:4–8

"Love . . . is not merely a feeling": C. S. Lewis, *Mere Christianity* (New York: HarperCollins, 1952), 100.

"This is my prayer: that your love": Philippians 1:9

"Rejoice in the wife of your youth": Proverbs 5:18–19

"I do, as I say": Robert Browning, "First Letter Robert Browning Wrote to Elizabeth Barrett Browning," *Udel.Edu*, 1845, https://sites.udel.edu/britlitwiki/elizabethandrobertbrowning/.

"How do I love thee": Elizabeth Barrett Browning, *Sonnets from the Portuguese* (New York: Dover Publications, 1850).

▨ CHAPTER 19: STRONG ENVIRONMENTS OF BLESSING

"You have to be stronger than these tormentors": Jon Tyson, *Beautiful Resistance* (Portland: Multnomah, 2020), 3–4.

"Overcome evil with good": Romans 12:21

"Train up a child in the way he should go": Proverbs 22:6 NKJV

"The Hebrew word translated 'train up'": Raymond Ortlund, Jr., *Proverbs: Wisdom that Works* (Wheaton, Illinois: Crossway, 2012), 154.

"Taste and see that the Lord is good": Psalm 34:8

"And when your children ask you": Exodus 12:26–27

"These commandments that I give you": Deuteronomy 6:6–7

"Jewish communities had a robust educational system": Mark Gerson, *The Telling: How Judaism's Essential Book Reveals the Meaning of Life* (New York: St. Martin's Essentials, 2021), 136–137.

"Listen, my son, to your father's instruction": Proverbs 1:8

"Bind them always on your heart": Proverbs 6:21

▨ CHAPTER 20: BLESS WHO?

"Love your enemies": Luke 6:27–28

"Do not repay anyone evil for evil": Romans 12:17–21

"Overcame a personal mistrust": Bill Keller, "Nelson Mandela, South Africa's Liberator as Prisoner and President, Dies at 95," *New York*

Times, December 5, 2013, https://www.nytimes.com/2013/12/06 /world/africa/nelson-mandela_obit.html.

"While we were God's enemies": Romans 5:10

We have now been given the "ministry of reconciliation": 2 Corinthians 5:18

■ CHAPTER 21: ONE NEW HUMANITY

"How good and pleasant it is when God's people": Psalm 133

"Now in Christ Jesus you who once were far away": Ephesians 2:13–16

"Citizens of heaven": Philippians 3:20 NLT

Not to judge each other over "disputable matters": Romans 14:1

"Here there is no Gentile or Jew": Colossians 3:11

"Therefore, as God's chosen people, holy and dearly loved": Colossians 3:12–14

"One new humanity": Ephesians 2:15

GRATITUDE

twenty-two

Thank You!

When God says, "Bless you," and then lavishes blessings on you, the only appropriate response is to receive His blessings gratefully and say back to Him often and with passion, "Thank You."

Remember the story of the ten lepers who were healed by Jesus? "One of them, when he saw he was healed, came back, praising God in a loud voice. He threw himself at Jesus' feet and thanked him." Then Jesus asked the obvious question: "Where are the other nine?" Well, the other nine, even though they had also been healed miraculously from a terribly disfiguring and contagious disease, had already moved on. This one guy received his healing and offered thanks.

I confess that if I am not careful, I can be more like the nine than the one. I receive something wonderful from God or from some other person, and I quickly start moving toward the next thing. I have to frequently remind myself how important it is to practice gratitude for what I already have—sometimes even to want what I already have. God does desire to bless us, but if we have a constant focus on future blessings, even promised blessings, we can miss the beauty of the already and the present. And it is just plain rude. God wants us to be thankful for what He has already done.

Because of what I understand of God's nature and His promises, I live with a high level of faith and expectancy for more good to be experienced in and through my life. I think this is mostly a positive thing; however, there is a fine line, at least for me. Several years ago, I suffered through a season of discouragement that bordered on depression. It was rooted in unmet expectations. Some things I had hoped for were not happening, at least not in the way I wanted, as fast as I wanted.

Then in my devotional time one morning, I came up against this psalm. "Lord, you alone are my inheritance, my cup of blessing. You guard all that is mine. The land you have given me is a pleasant land. What a wonderful inheritance!" I sensed God speaking to me.

Terry, am I not enough for you? I am your cup of blessing. I want you to be happy just with Me. Yet I have still blessed you with many other pleasant things. Your cup of blessing runs over. Before you ask for more, I want you to be able to say that I am enough and that what I have already given you is enough.

I began meditating on this, praying the words of this psalm and intentionally practicing gratitude each morning.

Sometime later Sharon said to me, "You seem to be feeling better. You seem encouraged. What happened?" I told her what I just told you. I shared that I was focused on who He is, on the blessing He is to me, on what He has already done and on what I already have. I told her that I had decided to quit moving so quickly toward more, and that I intended to come back and repeatedly and passionately say, "Thank You, thank You, thank You." And I was feeling better. A lot better.

The truth is that I have never been naturally gracious when it comes to receiving good things from others. This is particularly true when receiving a gift. I feel awkward and unworthy, and I never know quite what to say. Bad on me. My wife, on the other hand, could teach a master class on how to open a gift and make the gift giver feel as if they were the most thoughtful, generous and appreciated person in the world. She knows exactly how to act, what to say and how to express her heartfelt gratitude.

It occurs to me that God must really enjoy someone who knows how to receive Him and His blessings. Part of the deal with God is that we must get good at receiving, because He has given so much and has so much more He wants to give.

There is a memorable Scripture that asserts, "God loves a cheerful giver." I get this. If you are anything like me, you know that it is more blessed to give than to receive, and you absolutely love being on the giving side of things. This can be a kind of selfishness, however, because someone needs to experience the blessing of giving to you. Especially God.

Here is that passage with the next sentence included: "God loves a cheerful giver. And God is able to bless you abundantly, so that in all things at all times, having all that you need, you will abound in every good work." So God loves a cheerful giver, but He also loves a cheerful receiver. He does want you to happily give, but He also wants you to happily receive. Why? Because He wants to bless you abundantly.

I think some of us have such a sense of unworthiness it is hard for us to receive graciously. We only feel good when we feel bad. We open God's gifts and feel awkward at His generosity. Yet that is the thing about grace. He blesses you generously because of who He is, not because of who you are. Do you want to make Him feel good? Just say, "Thank You," and receive the good things He has done and is doing to you, in you and through you.

Do not say, "Oh no. Not me, I don't deserve this."

And also do not say, "Okay, got that. What is next?"

God loves a cheerful receiver. When we allow God to bless us, when we pause and express gratitude in response to His gifts, we help God experience the blessing of giving. It is like a blessing boomerang. He blesses us. We receive His blessing. He is blessed. He blesses us more. Give God pleasure. Accept His blessings and say, "Thanks!" with all your heart.

I like the idea that a human being can bless God. Again, we do this by receiving His blessings and by voicing our gratitude to Him through thanksgiving and praise. I see a magnificent example of this in the gospel of Luke when the angel Gabriel was sent by God to announce that the blessing of Jesus would come to the world in and through Mary. Jesus was God's desire to bless humanity wrapped up in the body of one person.

Everything about the announcement of His coming was electric with blessing. "The angel said to her, 'Rejoice, highly favored one, the Lord is with you; blessed are you among women.'" Then when Mary visited her cousin Elizabeth, the Holy Spirit caused Elizabeth to call Mary and her child blessed as well: "God has blessed you above all women, and your child is blessed. . . . You are blessed because you believed that the Lord would do what he said."

Mary received this. She accepted God's blessing and confessed that she was, in fact, blessed. And then she blessed God back. "Mary responded, 'Oh, how my soul praises the Lord. How my spirit rejoices in God my Savior!

. . . From now on all generations will call me blessed. For the Mighty One is holy, and he has done great things for me."

Blessing is reverberating everywhere in this story. God wants to bless all of humanity through Jesus. He blesses Mary. She receives His blessing through faith. She exuberantly praises Him, blessing Him back. Jesus is conceived in Mary, and she gives birth to the Ultimate Blessing, through whom all people in heaven and on earth will be blessed. Currents of supernatural blessing race back and forth, heaven to earth, earth to heaven, blessing the whole world.

It is amazing that when we receive God's blessing and say "thank You" through worship, we mere human beings can bless God. The writer to the Hebrews tells us that usually the "lesser is blessed by the greater." When we let the *greater* bless us, when we receive what He has promised and offer thanksgiving and praise, then we, the *lesser*, get to bless the *greater*. What a privilege and joy!

Revel with me in these immortal words: "Bless the LORD, O my soul; and all that is within me, bless His holy name! Bless the LORD, O my soul, and forget not all His benefits."

What blessing(s) do you need to receive and be grateful for today? How can you bless the Lord?

twenty-three

Join the Angel's Choir

Have you ever heard of a *complaints choir*? It seems too sad to be true, but there is such a thing—actually, a number of these things. A complaints choir is a group of people who write music to the lyrics of their complaints, and they perform their compositions with great passion and aggrieved expressions on their faces.

Complaints choirs have sprung up all over the world, from England to Singapore, from Australia to Finland. A wide range of grievances have been set to music as diverse as rhythm and blues in Philadelphia or an accordion, bass cello and tambourine ensemble in Tokyo. The singers belt out a voluminous array of uninspired complaints including, "I hate my job." "No one listens to me." "My boss makes his mistakes mine." "All of the good men are married." "I want my money back." Particularly grievous to me are lyrics from the very loud complainers in Philadelphia on our southern New Jersey border. They sing, "New Jersey drivers can't drive or park." Enough already!

I would much rather sing songs of gratitude, thank you. Imagine yourself singing complaints. How do you feel? Now juxtapose that with how you feel when you read these beautiful words from Colossians:

> Let the peace of Christ rule in your hearts. . . . And be thankful. . . . Admonish one another with all wisdom through psalms, hymns, and songs from the Spirit, singing to God with gratitude in your hearts. And whatever you do, whether in word or deed, do all in the name of the Lord Jesus, giving thanks to God the Father through him.

There. That feels so much better.

This is about more than how gratitude makes us feel, however. University of Southern California professor Robert A. Emmons does amazing work around the science of gratitude. His findings support the thread that we find in the Bible that extols the importance and advantages of gratitude. He writes that research reveals that blessings multiply when we count our blessings. There is "scientific proof that when people regularly engage in the systematic cultivation of gratitude, they experience a variety of measurable benefits."

These benefits include "higher levels of positive emotions such as joy, enthusiasm, love, happiness, and optimism" and higher levels of protection from "the destructive impulses of envy, resentment, greed, and bitterness." He intimates further that the disciplined practice of gratitude helps relieve stress, aids in healing and recovery from illness, supports strong physical health and enhances relationships. Emmons sums it up like this: "Gratitude, we have found, maximizes the enjoyment of the good—our enjoyment of others, of God, of our lives."

So you can choose to sing mournful songs of lament all day long, but complaining will only perpetuate the conditions about which you are complaining. Songs of gratitude, on the other hand, change you and have an impact on everything and everyone in your life in extraordinarily positive ways. Gratitude creates the conditions for blessing upon blessing.

This does not mean that we should ignore the challenges in our lives or the difficulties we face. It does mean, however, that it is infinitely advantageous to be thankful, but rarely useful to complain. The rare exceptions would include prayers that we see in some of the psalms where lament leads to hope-filled prayer and praise, or the need to bring a negative issue to the forefront to effect positive resolution and change.

There is a section of Scripture that has had a profound effect on my life. It is from Paul's writing to the Philippians:

> Don't worry about anything; instead pray about everything. Tell God what you need, and thank him for all he has done. Then you will experience God's peace, which exceeds anything that the human mind can understand.

I still remember the first time I practiced this with intention. I was eighteen years old, had suffered through what I thought was a life-altering setback and was riddled with anxiety. I read this Scripture and began to do what it says: Do not worry. Pray about everything with thanksgiving. Receive God's peace that transcends understanding. I experienced such relief. Even more, I witnessed God work in my life over the next several months. He answered my prayers of concern in ways beyond what I had asked or imagined.

Countless times, I daresay thousands of times since then, I have prayed through this Philippians passage and have reframed anxiety-inducing situations into opportunities for entreaty, gratitude and peace. I have not acted as though there was not a troubling situation nor that I did not need. I just presented my requests to God while expressing thanks for who He is, what He has already done and what I trust Him to do.

This passage goes on to say, "Fix your thoughts on what is true, and honorable, and right, and pure, and lovely, and admirable. Think about things that are excellent and worthy of praise." And this inexorably leads to another potent statement a few sentences later:

> I have learned how to get along happily whether I have much or little. . . . I can do everything God asks me to with the help of Christ who gives me the strength.

I perceive the secret of contentment in these Scripture passages. Do not be anxious. Be thankful. Make your requests known to God. Receive His peace in your heart and mind. Focus on the good and beautiful. Learn contentment in every situation. Flourish in every circumstance through Christ, who gives you strength.

Dr. Emmons writes, "Recognition is the quality that permits gratitude to be transformational. To recognize is to cognize, or think, differently about something from the way we have thought about it before." He also says that "thanking belongs to the realm of thinking." This is part of what these verses in Philippians teach us. We must deliberately *re-cognize*, or re-think, every circumstance in light of what we know about God and His promises.

You may experience something that provokes an instinctual complaint, but you can force yourself to reframe that circumstance in gratitude. You acknowledge that something is tempting you to worry, but you talk to God about it and bathe your prayer in thanksgiving. Your mind races to imagine negative possibilities, but you fix your thoughts on God and the good, and you receive the calming assurance that you will be blessed in every situation. You recognize that what may feel like a curse will no doubt end up as a blessing. And you absolutely refuse to focus on complaint.

I first read about the complaints choir during the Christmas season. My mind leapt to the lyrics of "O Come, All Ye Faithful." "Sing, choirs of angels, sing in exaltation. . . . O come, let us adore him, Christ the Lord." I want to join the angels' choir. I will not sing a song of complaint. I will join those in heaven and on earth who sing exultant songs of adoration and thanksgiving. Regardless of your circumstance, He alone is worthy. So sing, choirs of angels. Let's drown out the cacophony of negativity and complaints by "singing to God with gratitude in [our] hearts."

What area of complaint do you presently have that you need to rethink as an opportunity for gratitude and prayer?

twenty-four

Ingrates

G ratitude is so potent that the reverse is true as well, which is to say ingratitude is powerful, too. Be gently warned: Ingratitude has the negative potential to keep you from the blessings God wants so much for you.

When God's people were delivered from centuries of slavery in Egypt, they miraculously crossed the Red Sea, traveled to Mount Sinai and camped there about a year. They then began moving through the wilderness toward the Promised Land, the land God had promised them as part of His blessing to their father, Abraham. This journey should have taken a few months, but as you are surely aware, it took forty years. The reason it took so long and the reason so many died on the way is that God's people were ungrateful. Their thanklessness led to faithlessness. This exasperated God, and though He loved them ferociously, He would not bless them in their ingratitude.

Put bluntly, the vast majority of these folks were ingrates—ruthlessly thankless people—and God is not at all pleased when His people are ingrates. Here is part of the story. "The people complained about their hardships in the hearing of the LORD, and when he heard them his anger was aroused." God literally sent fire that burned among them until Moses, their leader, prayed it away. Then they complained about the wonder food, manna, that God provided every day.

> [They] began to crave other food, and again the Israelites started wailing and said, "If only we had meat to eat! We remember the fish we ate in Egypt at no cost—also the cucumbers, melons, leeks, onions and garlic. But now we have lost our appetite; we never see anything but this manna!"

Again, "The Lord became exceedingly angry." He caused quail to fall from the sky and pile up three feet deep and miles in every direction. When the people ate the quail, they were struck with a plague, and many died there. I have read that some of the incendiary language here is typical Near Eastern hyperbole of that time. It was used commonly to tell memorable stories and accentuate important points. Regardless of how one might walk this back, though, this much is clear: These people were championship-level complainers, and this displeased God greatly.

The consequence of this ingratitude was that they missed the blessings God had promised those who trust in Him. I think God was angry because He knew ingratitude would keep His children from enjoying the lives He had dreamed for them. Let me offer three observations about the power of grateful people, juxtaposed with the power of ingrate(ful) people:

First, grateful people please God and give life to others—ingrates displease God and take life from others. When these people complained, not only did God get upset, but their leader, Moses, was troubled as well. Moses prayed, "I cannot carry all these people by myself; the burden is too heavy for me. If this is how you are going to treat me, please go ahead and kill me." Ingratitude is not only ruinous for you, but it is also ruinous for the people around you. Moses decided he would rather die than live with such incorrigible complainers. Our ingratitude can be lethal for the people we love.

Being ungrateful is not just impolite; it is a vice, and it is murderously destructive. The great reformer Martin Luther believed that ingratitude was a profound spiritual failure and the root of all sin. In Romans, Paul indicts convincingly those who knew God, but "neither glorified him as God nor gave thanks to him, but their thinking became futile and their foolish hearts were darkened." Ingrates have power to destroy themselves and desperately damage others. We must surround ourselves with life-giving, grateful people. We must be life-giving, grateful people.

A second observation is that grateful people see the best in every circumstance—ingrates see the worst in everything. Manna was supernaturally amazing, but the ingrates missed the pleasures of God's provision. God provided this fresh bread every morning with the dew. Remarkably, it was able to be prepared with a variety of scintillating recipes, creating tastes as diverse as a bread and olive oil appetizer, or a cake for sweet dessert. "It tasted like something made with olive oil" and "tasted like wafers made with honey."

Bubba, from the movie *Forrest Gump*, comes to mind. As a shrimper, he loved optimistically enumerating all the ways that this one crustacean could be prepared.

Shrimp is the fruit of the sea. You can barbecue it, boil it, broil it, bake it, sauté it. There's shrimp-kebabs, shrimp Creole, shrimp gumbo. Pan-fried, deep-fried, stir-fried. There's pineapple shrimp, lemon shrimp, coconut shrimp, pepper shrimp, shrimp soup, shrimp stew, shrimp salad, shrimp and potatoes, shrimp burger, shrimp sandwich. That—that's about it.

Bubba was grateful for the multivarious possibilities of shrimp. Conversely, an ingrate can find something tasteless about anything. For the Israelites, the miracle manna was not onion-y enough, leek-y enough, garlicky enough, whatever enough. It also appears that they actually did have meat, since Pharaoh had given permission for them to take flocks and herds out of Egypt. There are other references to their livestock in the Exodus story as well.

Yet even the meat they had was not the meat they wanted. Tragically, they were just a short journey from the land flowing with milk and honey. Manna was not the end game; it was provision that God had created for a season. These ungrateful people missed more, better and best because they could not find a way to be thankful for this, here and now.

A third observation is that grateful people seize future possibilities—ingrates miss out on God's promises. Shortly after the story about these complainers and the plague, Moses sent twelve spies to explore the Promised Land. You know the story. Ten guys came back and spread a negative report about the gigantic battle necessary to take the land. Caleb and Joshua however, said the land they "explored is exceedingly good. If the LORD is pleased with us, he will lead us into that land . . . and will give it to us."

But of course, God was not pleased and could not do what He wanted because "the members of the community raised their voices and wept aloud. All the Israelites grumbled" and said they wanted to go back to Egypt. Such ingrates. Finally, God, so disappointed and done with their thanklessness, said, "In this wilderness your bodies will fall—every one of you twenty years old or more . . . who has grumbled against me." Lamentably, of all the "old enough to know better" Jews delivered from Egypt, only Caleb and Joshua entered the Promised Land of their father Abraham's blessing.

Research reveals that positive thoughts and emotions bathe our brains with chemicals that not only help us feel good but also to "think more quickly and creatively . . . and see and invent new ways of doing things." Gratitude helps us see and seize God's promised blessings. Ingratitude closes our hearts and eyes to possibility. Worse, unrelenting unthankfulness causes God to close His heart and eyes to us. As much as He wants to, God will not bless an ingrate.

Do you have an area of ingratitude in your life that you need to transition from grumbling to gratefulness?

twenty-five

In. All. Circumstances.

ere is a life-shaping scriptural directive that continues to confront and chasten me: "Give thanks in all circumstances; for this is God's will for you in Christ Jesus." I have looked at this every way I know how, and yet I keep coming back to the realization this means exactly what it says: Giving thanks in all circumstances is God's perfect will for me. I really need the Holy Spirit to help me with this.

Several years ago, Sharon and I were in Greece to do ministry and visit some notable historic sites. One evening, weary and at the end of a very busy week, we flew from Thessalonica to Athens. We were looking forward to a quiet dinner on our hotel veranda, which had a spectacular view of the Acropolis. It happened to be the night before the Athens Marathon, which was where the first marathon took place more than 2,500 years ago. All the roads around our hotel were closed. The closest our taxi could get was a mile and a half away.

It was a dreadfully hot night, but we walked through the packed streets of Athens dragging four large suitcases across ancient cobblestones with purses, briefcases and more hanging from every available appendage. And we got terribly lost. Phone reception was awful, and our map app, when we could access it, apparently delighted in pointing us in the wrong directions. I became agitated. Very agitated.

At some point while walking our own confused Athens Marathon, I felt liquid that had been dropped from above me splatter on my back and shoulder. At the same time, I heard a guy right behind me shout something in Greek while he was pointing up to a balcony. He rubbed his hand on my shirt, which came away with brown goop on it. He crinkled his nose, uttered a four-letter word in English that I will not repeat here and began wiping this stuff off me with a paper towel he just happened to have on his person. I realized something was awry, and we kept hold of our multitudinous baggage and walked away briskly.

When we finally found our hotel, me in my hot and very bothered condition, we learned that this brown goop thing was a regular scheme for the thieves who were standing by waiting to abscond with our luggage and other effects had we stopped moving to attend to the substance that had dropped from the sky (which ended up being some kind of paint). It did not take long to reflect on the bad that could have happened, to be grateful we were not robbed or otherwise injured, to realize we were still in Athens with a breathtaking view of the Acropolis just through our window and to know that all we had lost was a couple of hours, my paint-ruined clothing and regretfully, my temper.

Here is what bugs me about this story: I have mastered the art of rethinking a negative circumstance after I am no longer in the circumstance. My problem is that I have not mastered the art of being thankful while *in* an apparently negative circumstance. I am accomplished at seeing the blessing after the fact, but I am not so accomplished at seeing the blessing in the midst of the fact.

Thankfully, we are not told to be thankful *for* every circumstance. We are not to be thankful for evil things that happen, nor for injurious and damaging things. But we are to be thankful while we are in all circumstances. We must remember that, even before we are on the other side of difficulty, many times what appears to be bad news ends up being good news, that God truly is working everything together in our favor, that what the enemy meant for evil God will use for good and that ultimately every wrong thing in this world will be made right in the age to come.

In situations large and small, whether the loss of a job or something minor and relatively silly like being lost in Greece, we can find reasons to be thankful in circumstances we are not necessarily thankful for.

It is amazing what happens when we focus on blessings even in the face of challenge and need. I love the story Emerson Eggerichs tells about a woman who was challenged in her marriage who felt as if God impressed her "to imagine you are a giant highlighter, and . . . to highlight all those things that are honorable and true about your husband." She began to write down praiseworthy things about her husband and filled pages with an abundance of reasons she was grateful for him. And as she did, God renewed her love for him. We give oxygen to good and beautiful things when we focus on them. This is just how God designed life to work.

Paul practiced this methodology when he wrote to the Thessalonians. He had deep concerns about these new believers in the church who had been miraculously birthed in Thessalonica. He wrote pastoral letters to address his concerns and set some things in order, yet he focused relentlessly on the good things that were already happening in and through them.

> We always thank God for all of you and continually mention you in our prayers. We remember . . . your work produced by faith, your labor prompted by love, and your

endurance inspired by hope. . . . You became a model to all the believers.

He also told them, "You are our glory and joy." He followed it up by telling them, "Timothy has just now come to us from you and has brought good news about your faith and love." Paul stimulated spiritual growth by highlighting the good he was thankful for in the Thessalonians and promoting more of that good. "You yourselves have been taught by God to love each other. . . . We urge you, brothers and sisters, to do so more and more." He also reminded them, "We instructed you how to live in order to please God, as in fact you are living. Now we ask you and urge you . . . to do this more and more."

He encouraged them with, "We ought always to thank God for you, brothers and sisters, and rightly so, because your faith is growing more and more, and the love you have for one another is increasing." Do you want more of a good thing? Find the good in every situation, focus on the good you find, be relentlessly thankful for the good and good will grow and multiply.

Professor Kelly McGonigal, instructor of the acclaimed Stanford University course The Science of Willpower, posits that research reveals that when people focus on the negative in their lives, they open themselves to temptation, and they harm their ability to affect positive change. A dieter, for instance, who in a weak moment indulges in a piece of chocolate cake and focuses on their failure, is more likely to spiral into further hedonic indulgence. She calls this (forgive me, but this is a term of science in this context) "the what-the-hell effect." She writes, "What the hell, I already blew my diet. I might as well eat the whole thing." She says, "The brain, it turns out, is especially susceptible to temptation when we're feeling bad."

I think this principle is true in many areas of life. When we concentrate on the negative, the weakness, the failure, what we do not have and so on, we plummet into more negativity and close ourselves to good and God. I propose that we activate the "what-the-heaven effect." We can look for good in every situation, shine our mind's spotlight on the good and give copious thanks for the good. We must focus on the heavenly, not the hellacious, and we should expect heaven to help us when we do. When we give thanks in every circumstance, we are doing the will of God.

So count your blessings. Go ahead, count them one by one, and watch as God gives you more and more blessings to count.

Do you have a negative circumstance in your life in which you need to be more intentionally thankful?

twenty-six

Temporary Darkness

Thomas Alva Edison is one of the most consequential people in history. During his 84 years, he acquired 1,093 patents and innovated a wide diversity of inventions, including the phonograph and motion pictures. Yet his most significant contribution to humanity was when he harnessed energy and conducted electricity through wire to turn on an incandescent lightbulb. He then worked out how to conduct electricity to burn multiple lights, and eventually, along with some other innovators, brought electricity and light to most of the developed world in a relatively few years. He gave people across the world the ability to dispel darkness with the flip of a switch. This explains why during his lifetime, he was the most celebrated person on the planet. He brought light to a dark world.

When Edison died in 1931, 52 years after he first caused a light to viably burn, it was suggested to the president of the United States that the entire electrical system, and all the lights in the nation, be turned off for one minute to honor him. The president realized, however, "that such a gesture would immobilize the nation and quite possibly kill countless people." It was decided that they would only ask private individuals and companies to turn off their lights as Edison was buried.

The entire nation paused as lights were still turned off seemingly everywhere and as network radio stations played "Haydn's setting of the words of Genesis, darkness was upon the face of the deep." And in those few minutes, as much of the nation experienced darkness, it became starkly obvious how desperately the world needed Edison's light. They could not go back to the dark that was before.

In Scripture, *darkness* describes the chaos that existed before God brought light. It is also used as a metaphor for evil. I love the glorious words in the gospel of John that tell us in Jesus "there was Life and this Life was the Light of the human race. And this Light shines on in the darkness, and the darkness did not put it out." In Jesus, God harnessed the energy that caused and sustains the universe—life itself!—into the body of one man. That one man brought light to a dark world.

Darkness tried to put the light out. For a period, it looked as if darkness succeeded. When Jesus was crucified, "darkness came over the whole land" for hours. While He was buried, light went out all over this planet. But that darkness was temporary—it lasted only three days. Because of His resurrection, darkness is always only temporary. "The light shines in the darkness, and the darkness can never extinguish it."

Let's tackle this head-on, though: There are times when it feels as though darkness lasts forever, as though light has been extinguished for good. We live in an often-dark world, and we face dark realities: death, disease, pain, mental illness, tragedy and all kinds of loss. This is the darkness at the extreme edges of the "all circumstances" that we discussed in the last chapter. These are situations so dark that it is difficult to see our blessings to be able to count them and so dark that gratitude is difficult to feel and express. The light *is* shining, but without question, it is shining in the darkness.

Jesus understands this and is with us in this. I love the story of the sickness, death and resurrection of His friend Lazarus and His relationship with his sisters, Mary and Martha. Jesus received an urgent message telling Him that Lazarus was sick, and He was asked to please come quickly. He waited in place for two days even though He "really did love Martha and this sister of hers and Lazarus." Jesus knew this sickness would not end in death but would bring glory to God and blessing to people; therefore, He allowed an apparently bad thing to happen. Lazarus died. Sometimes when Jesus loves us, He waits. He allows us to encounter dark things for reasons only He understands.

One of these reasons is that He wants us to learn to trust Him. By the time Jesus arrived, Lazarus had already been in the tomb four days. Martha, who was understandably distraught, went to meet Him and said, "If you had been here my brother would not have died. But even now I know whatever you ask God, God will give it to you." Jesus told her Lazarus would be raised from the dead and that any "person believing into me, even when that person dies, will live again." He asked Martha, "Do you believe this?" She answered that she did.

The word *believe* in this context should be thought of as "trust." To believe in Jesus, especially in a dark situation, is more than believing He exists. It is trusting that He is who He says He is and that He will do what He said He will do. This was a critical moment for Martha. She trusted Jesus in the midst of her loss and disappointment. She was grateful for His presence. She did not understand what He was doing, but she "believed into Him" nevertheless.

Then Mary showed up crying, and Jesus "was greatly troubled in spirit and deeply moved." As Frederick Dale Bruner translates it, "Jesus bawled." What a paradox!

Jesus knew that the story had a happy ending and that the darkness they faced was only temporary, yet He entered into the suffering of those He loved. In the same way, He enters our suffering "to empathize with our weaknesses."

He knows what it is to confront the darkness that wanted to destroy Him and to offer desperate "prayers and pleadings, with a loud cry and tears, to the one who could deliver him out of death" before He was delivered from death through resurrection. He knows what it is to suffer. He feels your pain, and He could not possibly care more, even though He knows your story will end well. Jesus did not just weep, however. "He roared with a great voice, 'Lazarus come out of there.'" And Lazarus did.

Most of the dark things I have dealt with in my life have been resolved with a *Jesus roars* moment—a prayer so powerfully answered or a need so profoundly met that it feels as if a dead person has come alive again. Then there are things I face when I know He is with me and cares for me, but for whatever His reason, I am still waiting. I am left to trust Him and am called to practice gratitude in a situation in which it feels as though darkness is winning.

As I write these words, my dad suffers from Alzheimer's disease, I have a dear parishioner who is not yet healed from ALS but in the meantime is wasting away, and I officiated this week at the funeral of an irreplaceable friend. That is just to name a few of the darknesses in my life that are yet unresolved.

We must remember that every dark thing in our lives and in this world will be resolved ultimately when a "loud shout from the throne" and a trumpet blast from heaven will generate the resurrection of all believers to new life in a new heaven and a new earth. I am struck by the fact that although Lazarus was resurrected, he did die again and is now, with all believers who have gone before, waiting for Jesus to roar again and renew all things once and for all. In that new world, the light will not shine in darkness because darkness will be no more. "And there will be no night there—no need for lamps or sun—for the Lord God will shine on them."

I promise you, whatever darkness you face is only temporary. Live with an expectation of present victory. Know without a doubt that you will have complete and total triumph in the brightly shining world to come. I encourage you to practice a trusting gratitude even in present darkness. The Light does still shine brightly, even here.

Will you "continually offer the sacrifice of praise to God . . . giving thanks to His name," even when you face dark situations?

twenty-seven

Give It Back

This might surprise you, but when God gives you blessings, He expects you to be willing to give them back.

When I was a teenager, my sister and I wrote songs and played music and performed in a number of churches and other venues. She was—and is—a sensational vocalist and keyboardist. I was a decent enough vocalist and bassist, and I worked really hard at playing guitar not all that well. An extraordinarily generous man who appreciated my passionate effort took me to a music store and bought me a beautiful and expensive Fender Stratocaster electric guitar. I cherished that quintessential guitar as a prized possession, a gift from God.

In my early thirties and early in my pastorate, I called my then-small congregation to give sacrificial gifts to raise the funds to purchase and remodel our first church building. Since I did not have much to give in that season of life, an unintended consequence of my call to the congregation was that I felt called by the Holy Spirit to sell my precious Stratocaster and give the money to the church.

It was as if God said, *I used that generous guy to give this to you, and now I want it back*. It was not easy at first, but I sold my guitar and gave the money to the church. When I did, I actually felt great.

Then, as my oldest son, Caleb, reached his teenage years, he developed into a skilled musician, primarily a guitarist. We purchased an inexpensive electric guitar for him, and he played it to great effect, leading a band of other talented kids who served our church's youth group and beyond. I confess to thinking, *It sure would have been nice to have been able to give him my Stratocaster*. No regret, mind you, but a thought that I had more than once.

Then one day, a guy who knew none of this said to me, "I am so impressed with Caleb. I make custom electric guitars much better than anything you could purchase in any music store. I would really like to craft a guitar exclusively for him, if that's okay with you."

My son ended up with a guitar that was even nicer than that classic Stratocaster. He still plays it much better than I ever played mine. I learned then that sometimes God gives you a gift, asks for it back and then regifts you with much more than you ever gifted Him.

There is rich and fresh scholarship that brings important perspective to what gift-giving, or grace, meant in the Greco-Roman and Jewish worlds. These were the worlds that framed the linguistic and cultural context of the New Testament. "Namely, in the ancient world gift and grace entailed reciprocity, at least on the level of gratitude but often in the sense of reciprocal gift-giving."

This means that in the first century a person would give a gift to someone with the anticipation of receiving back from them. At a minimum, they would expect gratitude, but they also would expect a gift of corresponding value back. God's grace gifted to us in Jesus is unique in that He saved us in spite of the fact that our worth is nothing compared to His, nor are we able to reciprocate anything approaching equal value. But it is similar in that having saved us, He does expect us to give Him something valuable back.

What does He expect back? Our whole lives in general, and everything and anything in our lives in particular. The apostle Paul captured this expectation when he wrote, "I urge you, brothers and sisters, in view of God's mercy, to offer your bodies as living sacrifices," and "It is by grace you have been saved, through faith . . . it is the gift of God. . . . For we are God's handiwork, created in Christ Jesus to do good works."

God gives us life, and He wants our lives back. He gives us gifts, and He wants us to employ those gifts in His service. He gives us treasure, and He wants us to make those treasures available to Him for His work. He gives us blessings, and He wants us to be conduits of blessing to others. He does want us to say thank-you, but much more than that, He wants us to offer Him back everything we are and have.

In His signature teaching in the gospel of Luke, Jesus taught us to live with an exceptional generosity of spirit in response to who we are in Him and the kindness He has lavished on us.

> "Live generously. . . . Live out this God-created identity the way our Father lives toward us, generously and graciously. . . . Give away your life; you'll find life given back, but not merely given back—given back with bonus and blessing. Giving, not getting, is the way. Generosity begets generosity."

Jesus calls us to a high-minded, wholehearted, open-handed, big-inside benevolence in our approach to Him, to His people and to all of life. God has blessed us so much in so many ways, and He wants us to be as radically generous as He is to us. And when we are, we always end up with more—God blesses us more, and people bless us more.

Do you remember how Jesus fed more than five thousand people with five loaves of bread and two fish? That food came from a little boy who had been blessed with provisions for his lunch and who offered it to Jesus, who "took the five loaves and the two fish, looked up toward heaven, and blessed them." He then multiplied what He had been given, fed the multitude and ended up with twelve baskets of leftovers.

This is what happens when we take what we have been given and give it back to God. He blesses it, makes more of it, uses it to bless others and makes sure we always end up with more than what we offered. More! Always more!

If you want this generosity-begets-generosity reality, blessings reciprocated from God to us, from us to God, from us to people, and people back to us, you must think *abundance*. Thoughts of abundance should be our default setting. The psalmist exclaimed, "We went through fire and water, but you brought us to a place of abundance." An abundance mindset focuses on plenty. "The LORD is my shepherd, I lack nothing." God, the Creator, never runs out and is always capable of creating more. He gives us creative power and the ability to make more in many ways.

A mind that is bathed in abundance inspires a perspective of possibility, potential, expectations of favor and having more than enough. A person with an abundance mentality is extravagantly generous because they know they will never run out of love, forgiveness, gifts, opportunities and blessings of all kinds. "One person gives freely, yet gains even more; another withholds unduly, but comes to poverty. A generous person will prosper; whoever refreshes others will be refreshed."

I cannot help but think about the fabulous language in the inspired words of the prophet Malachi, who warned people not to "rob God" by withholding tithes and offerings. He wrote that God wanted His people to stop robbing Him and to "bring the whole tithe. . . . and see if I will not throw open the floodgates of heaven and pour out so much blessing that there will not be room enough to store it."

God is saying that if you do not give what He asked you for, you are robbing Him of the opportunity to take it in His hands and use it for His purposes, to bless it, to multiply it and to give you back more than you can even imagine. This principle applies to everything we are and have by God's grace. Do not rob God of the pleasure of opening the windows of heaven to bless you. Be willing to give Him whatever He asks for.

Is there anything you have been given that you have been unwilling to offer back to God?

twenty-eight

The Blessed God

As we reach the end of this journey together, I am overwhelmed with gratitude for one overarching thought: God is blessed, and He invites you and me to share in His blessedness.

I have long been fascinated by the apostle Paul's description of the good news about Jesus as the "gospel concerning the glory of the blessed God." Blessed is God's state of being. He is inexplicably content and lives in an eternal condition of joyous well-being. One translation of this passage speaks of "the glorious gospel of the blissful God" and another as "the glory of the happy God." When you are able to see God as blissfully happy and utterly blessed, you cannot help but live every moment with an expectation that God wants to bless you, to be in harmonious relationship with you and to do good to you, in you and through you.

Jonathan Edwards was a pastor, theologian and some say America's greatest philosopher. He was a revivalist, he was a leader of the Great Awakening of 1742, and when he died, he was the president of Princeton University. Edwards wrote a book in which he attempted to explain why God created the world. In brief, he said that God did not need anything because He was perfectly happy in Himself. He was everything good, true and beautiful.

But God wanted to share Himself, to show His glory—who He is and what He does. So He created this universe and put people in it so He could expand Himself, multiply Himself and gain a greater audience for Himself. Edwards wrote that everything that exists in the cosmos, and particularly human beings, exists for this purpose. God is so blessed that He wanted a whole universe to enjoy Him forever!

Try to imagine God's immense happiness, then, in creation. Every time He added another dimension to this world, God "saw that it was good." Scripture indicates that God's exhilaration in creation was so all-encompassing that innumerable angels celebrated His pleasure and "shouted for joy."

When God created human beings, He was full of unmitigated delight and "saw all that he had made and it was very good." Then what did the blessed God do? "God blessed them" and invited them to join Him in His life and His work. I think God was ecstatic! He had created the entire universe so that He could share His happiness with men and women, people like you and me.

I know Adam sneezed. I know humanity fell sick. I know sin plagued God's plan. This where the Good News about Jesus comes in. It is "the gospel concerning the glory of the blessed God." Jesus came to reverse the curse and bring the blessing back to heal us and this world from the disease of sin. God sent Jesus to ensure He will have in the end what He inaugurated in the beginning, which is a blessed God in relationship with blessed people. Jesus said that those of us who believe in Him and follow Him will experience "the renewal of all things" in the age to come, or literally "genesis again." We taste this future hope in our lives now when we walk with Jesus.

There is a revealing line in a story Jesus tells about how He rewards people who have partnered with Him in His work. He invites them to "come and share your master's happiness." This is what He has been about from the very beginning. This is what He is about right now. The blessed God wants you to share in His happiness.

It really is this simple: If you will let Him, if you will cooperate with God's good intentions, He will bless you. That blessing will be manifest in your life in every way. The very first psalm is explicit: "Blessed is the one ... whose delight is in the law of the Lord. ... Whatever they do prospers." God delights when we delight in Him and His Word. He is elated when He can prosper us in everything we do.

Do you remember the classic Hellenic myth of King Midas? He had everything a king could want, and he shared his profligate life with his daughter, Zoe, or *life*. Favored by Dionysus, the god of celebration, Midas was granted one wish to receive anything his heart desired. In an instant, he said he wished that everything he touched would turn to gold.

The next morning, he touched his bedside table and it turned to gold. Midas excitedly went through his castle touching furniture and walls. Gold. But then he saw a beautiful rose and took it in his hands to smell its fragrance and it turned to gold. He tried to eat a grape. Gold. Bread. Gold. Then his daughter ran to him unknowingly and joyously, and before he could warn her, she threw herself on him to hug him. Zoe turned to gold as well.

Midas, rich beyond imagination and miserable beyond comprehension, begged to be released from the Midas touch. He pleaded, "I want life, not gold." Dionysus had mercy and told Midas he could be released from this strange gift if he would give up all the gold in his kingdom. Midas gladly turned his gold back into the things they were designed to be, gave away his possessions and rejoiced with his daughter in the vibrance of life and things more precious than gold.

If God told you today that you could pray one prayer concerning yourself and it would be immediately answered, what would you pray for? I would ask Him to do for me the very first thing He did for the very first human beings: I would ask Him to bless me. I know if He blesses me, then everything I am will be blessed, every person I touch will be blessed and everything I put my hand to will be blessed.

A lot of people might ask for some version of the Midas touch without thinking. I want the blessing touch. I believe God wants everything in our lives to turn into blessing.

I thrill at the words of Moses to God's children as they journeyed to the Promised Land. He told them that if they would walk with God, if they would do what He said, that "all these blessings will come on you and accompany you." He then enumerated multitudinous blessings that they should anticipate. I believe that we should expect them as well. After all, the New Testament assures us that the blessing of Abraham and his seed are ours through Jesus Christ.

Here are some of the blessings God promised His children through Moses in Deuteronomy 28: You will be blessed wherever you live; you will be blessed wherever you go; your children will be blessed; your business will be blessed; your finances will be blessed; your ministry will be blessed; you will be blessed in everything you put your hand to; people—even your enemies—will see that you are blessed and reverence God and respect you; and "the LORD will grant you abundant prosperity . . . and open the heavens . . . to bless all the work of your hands."

According to some renderings of this passage, blessings will find you, overtake you and chase you down. Everything in your life, everything you touch—blessing!

I have said this every way I know how, and I literally tremble with conviction as I write these last few words. If you believe in Him and are in relationship with Him and will let Him help you do what He says, the blessed God will bless you in every imaginable way.

I now offer this ancient, anointed and sacred prayer: "The LORD bless you and keep you; the LORD make his face shine on you and be gracious to you; the LORD turn his face toward you and give you peace." Amen.

Do you believe with everything in you that God wants to bless you?

SECTION 4 NOTES

▧ CHAPTER 22: THANK YOU!

"Where are the other nine?": Luke 17:15–19

"Lᴏʀᴅ, you alone are my inheritance": Psalm 16:5–6 ɴʟᴛ

"God loves a cheerful giver.": 2 Corinthians 9:7–8

"The angel said to her, 'Rejoice, highly favored one'": Luke 1:28 ɴᴋᴊᴠ

"God has blessed you above all women": Luke 1:42–45 ɴʟᴛ

"Mary responded, 'Oh, how my soul praises the Lord'": Luke 1:46–49 ɴʟᴛ

"Lesser is blessed by the greater": Hebrews 7:7

"Bless the Lord, O my soul; and all that is within me": Psalm 103:1–2 ɴᴋᴊᴠ

▧ CHAPTER 23: JOIN THE ANGEL'S CHOIR

"New Jersey drivers can't drive or park": Phyllis Korkki, "Turning Complaints Into Art," *New York Times*, December 8, 2009, https://www.nytimes.com/2009/12/09/arts/music/09complaint.html.

"Let the peace of Christ rule in your hearts": Colossians 3:15–17

"Higher levels of positive emotions such as joy": Robert A. Emmons, *Thanks!: How Practicing Gratitude Can Make You Happier* (New York: HarperCollins, 2008).

"Don't worry about anything; instead pray": Philippians 4:6–7 ɴʟᴛ

"Fix your thoughts on what is true, and honorable, and right": Philippians 4:8 ɴʟᴛ

"I have learned how to get along happily": Philippians 4:11–13 ᴛʟʙ

"Recognition is the quality that permits gratitude": Robert A. Emmons, *Thanks!: How Practicing Gratitude Can Make You Happier* (New York: HarperCollins, 2008).

"O Come, All Ye Faithful": John Frances Wade, "O Come, All Ye Faithful," 1841, https://hymnary.org/text/o_come_all_ye_faithful_joyful _and_triump.

"Singing to God with gratitude in [our] hearts": Colossians 3:16

CHAPTER 24: INGRATES

"The people complained about their hardships": Numbers 11:1–34

"I cannot carry all these people by myself": Numbers 11:14

The great reformer Martin Luther believed that ingratitude: R. A. Emmons and T. T. Kneezel, "Giving Thanks: Spiritual and Religious Correlates of Gratitude," *Journal of Psychology and Christianity*, 24(2) (2005), 140–148.

"Neither glorified him as God": Romans 1:21

"It tasted like something made with olive oil": Numbers 11:8

"Tasted like wafers made with honey": Exodus 16:31

"Shrimp is the fruit of the sea": Robert Zemeckis, *Forrest Gump*, Hollywood, CA, Paramount Pictures, 1994.

"If the Lord is pleased with us, he will lead us into that land": Numbers 14:7–8

"The members of the community raised their voices and wept aloud": Numbers 14:1

"In this wilderness your bodies will fall": Numbers 14:29

"Think more quickly and creatively": Shawn Achor, *The Happiness Advantage* (New York: Currency, 2010), 44.

CHAPTER 25: IN. ALL. CIRCUMSTANCES.

"Give thanks in all circumstances": 1 Thessalonians 5:18

"To imagine you are a giant highlighter": Emerson Eggerichs, *The 4 Wills of God* (Nashville: B&H Books, 2018), 93.

"We always thank God for all of you": 1 Thessalonians 1:2–3, 7

"You are our glory and joy":1 Thessalonians 2:20

"Timothy has just now come to us from you": 1 Thessalonians 3:6

"You yourselves have been taught by God to love each other": 1 Thessalonians 4:9–10

"We instructed you to live in order to please God": 1 Thessalonians 4:1

"Because your faith is growing more and more": 2 Thessalonians 1:3

"The what-the-hell effect": Kelly McGonigal, *The Willpower Instinct* (New York: Avery, 2013), 144, 135.

▓ CHAPTER 26: TEMPORARY DARKNESS

"That such a gesture would immobilize the nation": Edmund Morris, *Edison* (New York: Random House, 2019), 632.

"Haydn's setting of the words of Genesis": Morris, *Edison*, 631.

"There was Life and this Life was the Light": Frederick Dale Bruner, *The Gospel of John: A Commentary* (Grand Rapids, MI: Eerdmans, 2012), 664.

"Darkness came over the whole land": Luke 23:44

"The light shines in the darkness": John 1:5 NLT

"If you had been here my brother would not have died"; "Person believing into me"; "Do you believe this?": Bruner, *The Gospel of John*, 664.

"Was greatly troubled in spirit and deeply moved": Bruner, *The Gospel of John*, 674.

"To empathize with our weaknesses": Hebrews 4:15

"Prayers and pleadings, with a loud cry and tears": Hebrews 5:7 NLT

"He roared with a great voice": Bruner, *The Gospel of John*, 681.

"Loud shout from the throne": Revelation 21:3 NLT

"And there will be no night there": Revelation 22:5 NLT

"Continually offer the sacrifice of praise to God . . . giving thanks to His name": Hebrews 13:15 NKJV

▓ CHAPTER 27: GIVE IT BACK

"Namely, in the ancient world gift and grace": Scot McKnight, *The Letter to the Colossians* (Grand Rapids, MI: Eerdmans, 2018), 48.

"I urge you, brothers and sisters": Romans 12:1

"It is by grace you have been saved, through faith": Ephesians 2:8–10

"Live generously. . . . Live out this God-created identity": Luke 6:27–38 MSG

"Took the five loaves and the two fish": Luke 9:16 NLT

"We went through fire and water": Psalm 66:11

"The Lord is my shepherd, I lack nothing": Psalm 23:1

"One person gives freely, yet gains even more": Proverbs 11:24–25

"Bring the whole tithe": Malachi 3:10

■ CHAPTER 28: THE BLESSED GOD

"Gospel concerning the glory of the blessed God": 1 Timothy 1:11

"The glorious gospel of the blissful God": American Bible Union, *The New Testament of Our Lord and Savior Jesus Christ* (New York: American Bible Union, 1866).

"The glory of the happy God": Joseph Bryant Rotherham, *Rotherham's Emphasized Bible* (Grand Rapids, MI: Kregel Publications, 1959).

Edwards wrote a book: Ben Stevens, ed., *Why God Created the World: A Jonathan Edwards Adaptation* (Colorado Springs: NavPress, 2014).

"Saw that it was good": Genesis 1:10

"Shouted for joy": Job 38:7

"Saw all that he had made and it was very good": Genesis 1:31

"God blessed them" and invited them: Genesis 1:28

"It is the gospel concerning the glory of the blessed God": 1 Timothy 1:11

"The renewal of all things" in the age to come: Matthew 19:28

"Genesis again": John Eldredge, *All Things New: Heaven, Earth, and the Restoration of Everything You Love* (Nashville: Thomas Nelson, 2017), 13.

"Come and share your master's happiness": Matthew 25:23

"Blessed is the one . . . whose delight": Psalm 1:1–3

The classic Hellenic myth of King Midas: "King Midas," *GreekMythology.com*, 2021, https://www.greekmythology.com/Myths/Mortals/King_Midas/king_midas.html.

"All these blessings will come on you": Deuteronomy 28:2

"The Lord will grant you abundant prosperity": Deuteronomy 28:11–12

"The Lord bless you and keep you": Numbers 6:24–26

Acknowledgments

While writing this book about blessing, I have been blessed in so many ways by so many people. Here are just a few:

I am blessed by the amazing people of The Life Christian Church. You are the incubator for much of what I have learned, experienced, witnessed, taught and written about what it means to be blessed. I hope to have the privilege to pray "the Lord bless you" benediction over you for many years to come and to bless you in many other ways, as well. You have brought abundant blessings to me and my family over these years. To all and each of you, and especially to our board and elders, a huge thank-you.

I am blessed to serve with a wonderful staff team. Your partnership and each of you doing your jobs with such effectiveness allows me to do things like write this book.

I am extremely grateful for you. Special thanks to my executive assistant, Najja Couch. You were with me every step of this project, and I could not have written this book without you. Sharon and I appreciate you very much.

I am blessed to have Esther Feddorkevich as my agent. Esther, you are a positive force of nature. Thank you for believing in me and my work and for making this project happen. And thanks to the entire team at The Fedd Agency for your always excellent work.

I am blessed to have the opportunity to partner with the wonderful team at Chosen. Special thanks to Kim Bangs for being such an effective advocate for this message. You went the extra mile to make sure this book was published successfully, and I am very grateful. And to my editor Lori Janke, thank you for significantly improving my work.

I am blessed by those who read an early manuscript and gave me great feedback. What a group! Maria Bellamy, Dan Dean, Russ Hammonds, Amanda Smith, Caleb Smith, Christian Smith, Sumerr Smith and Lauren Steckley: I am deeply appreciative of your investment of time and for your incisive insights. Without question, you made this a much better book.

I am blessed to be married to the love of my life, Sharon. I am filled with gratitude for the blessing of sharing all of life with you. Thank you for letting me read early chapter drafts to you at all hours of the day and night and for your intuitive wisdom. I love you more than I can possibly express. And together we are extraordinarily blessed with our kids, who bring us such joy. Sumerr, Caleb and Lindsay, and Christian and Amanda   I love each of you with all of my heart.

I am blessed beyond measure by God and His grace. Lord, I am overwhelmed by Your desire to bless a guy like me. I am grateful beyond words for the many ways I experience Your blessing every day. Thank You for more and better life than I ever dreamed of.

Terry A. Smith has served as lead pastor of The Life Christian Church in the New York City/New Jersey metropolitan area for thirty years. He has been married to Sharon for nearly forty years, and they have three adult children: Sumerr, Caleb and Christian, and daughters-in-law Lindsay and Amanda. Terry is the author of *The Hospitable Leader: Create Environments Where People and Dreams Flourish* and *Live Ten: Jump-Start the Best Version of Your Life*.

A gifted communicator, Terry speaks in a variety of venues nationally and internationally to inspire people to discover and pursue the life God dreams for them. Learn more at www.TerryASmith.com and www.tlcc.org. He can also be found on Twitter, Facebook, Instagram or YouTube (www.TerryASmith.com/social).